TAMING THE
SALES MGMNT
BEAST NOW
AUG 2008
SUNNYVALE CA
SJK

Magic Numbers for Sales Management

Key measures to Evaluate Sales Success

Magic Numbers for Sales Management

Key measures to Evaluate Sales Success

John Davis

John Wiley & Sons (Asia) Pte Ltd.

Other Wiley Editorial Offices

John Wiley & Sons, 111 River Street, Hoboken, NJ 07030, USA
John Wiley & Sons, The Atrium Southern Gate, Chichester PO19 8SQ, England
John Wiley & Sons (Canada) Ltd, 5353 Dundas Street West, Suite 400, Toronto, Ontario M9B 6HB, Canada
John Wiley & Sons Australia Ltd, 42 McDougall Street, Milton, Queensland 4064, Australia
Wiley-VCH, Boschstrasse 12, D-69469 Weinheim, Germany

Library of Congress Cataloging-in-Publication Data

ISBN-13 978 0 470-82187-9
ISBN-10 0-470-82187-6

Typeset in 12/14 points, Times Roman by C&M Digitals (P) Ltd.
Printed in Singapore by Saik Wah Press Pte Ltd
10 9 8 7 6 5 4 3 2 1

To my brothers, Steve and Peter—you have
been my lifelong inspirations.

Contents

Acknowledgments

I started out in sales early in my career and loved it. As I took on more marketing responsibilities leading global marketing teams, the early sales techniques I learned proved invaluable as my career grew. From the hard-to-measure, yet absolutely critical people skills, to rigorous planning and goal setting, sales provided my first lessons in business.

This is my third book with John Wiley & Sons. Nick Wallwork has been a great help with each project and an enthusiastic supporter. His wry wit and relentless energy are refreshing and motivating, and he is supported by a great team, particularly, Janis Soo. Janis has guided much of the day-to-day support I have received from Wiley, from marketing ideas to working with the copyeditors. She has been an enthusiastic and thoughtful supporter on this and my previous books. As with some of my previous work, Brickwork Consultancy provided research support on several key metrics. Shashank Nigam, a bright and ambitious student at Singapore Management University, was instrumental in both this and my previous book, *Marketing Measures: 103 Metrics Every Marketer Must Know*, spending countless hours on research. While many colleagues provided helpful input, Don Skloss, who has led sales teams at Kraft General Foods, Transamerica, Dean Foods and Resers, offered thoughtful and detailed guidance about the sales process and measures throughout the sales cycle. I have also been the recipient of great advice from mentors who took the time to work with me throughout my career, and I have worked alongside some of the best sales minds in business. From Woodside Hotels to Nike to Transamerica to Informix and including my own start-ups, the professionals in those organizations have been a source of ceaseless inspiration. In the past few years, both in the United States and Asia, I have had the good fortune to work with and study over 100 companies, talking to their leaders and spending time with field-based management. Their insights helped shape the content of this book as well. John Owen, the editor, has worked with me twice now and provides essential, clarifying guidance, particularly with hard-to-explain concepts.

My wife, Barb, and my kids Katie, Chris and Bridget are the reason my books were written at all. They allowed me the time to write and encouraged me every step of the way. While it sounds like a cliché, I am indeed the luckiest guy on earth.

Introduction

Sales management and field sales activities are critical to business success. Without talented sales people, most organizations would struggle. Senior managers and managers working in the main operations, away from the sales force, do not see the daily challenges confronting their sales people. Often, operational employees do not even know who the sales people are, which is a shame since sales people are the face of the company to the customer. Equally important, many sales people are located away from corporate headquarters, traveling constantly and rarely, if ever, meeting with their home-office colleagues. Since the operations people are responsible for fulfilling the orders generated by the sales force, sales representatives must make the effort to connect with their corporate counterparts. Given the daily demands on every employee, this two-way communication, as simple as it sounds, is hard to accomplish. Nevertheless, striving to improve this would undoubtedly reap benefits for the organization financially and socially, breaking down barriers of misunderstanding and improving communication across the board. Customers would benefit, too, of course.

Shedding light on how sales people perform is a good step toward better corporate communication. For sales management and their field sales representatives, measuring performance is vital to company success. As with marketing activities, there is no universal formula which either measures sales performance or perfectly forecasts the future. Selling is complex, with significant demands placed on individual sales representatives and teams to deliver the revenues forecast by the company. Top-performing sales reps must do many things well. They have to have a thorough knowledge of their products and of the competitive environment in which they are operating. They have to understand customers and their needs. This requires effective consultation, communication and time-management skills that will help to build long-lasting, profitable relationships with customers. They also have to be able to work closely with their own company's managers to ensure smooth delivery and support of products and services in a way that both satisfies the customer's expectations and meets company goals each year. This necessitates careful planning and record keeping. They need to be able to develop financial arguments that convince customers and their own finance people. And, of course, they have to be able to withstand regular rejection.

This list is by no means exhaustive. Suffice to say that the job of sales people is hard. Much of the success in selling is the result of subjective activities, such as the art of persuasion, none of which have a perfectly formed formula that prescribes the perfect behavior every time. These subjective factors are challenging to measure.

Sales forces conducting person-to-person selling remain one of the most effective ways to market products. The costs are higher due to the limited number of customers a sales person can reach in comparison with the broad-based reach of integrated marketing communications. Nevertheless, business is still conducted primarily based on relationships between companies and customers, so sales people play a critical role.

Sales people uncover the needs of buyers, whether retail buyers, wholesalers, B2B buying teams or individual consumers in retail stores. The best sales people are those who have a unique combination of business intelligence, entrepreneurial spirit, strong people skills and an intense desire to win.

Success in selling is a relationship-driven process, however. No matter how elegant or sophisticated the quantitative analysis, closing the sale depends on interpersonal relationships, in which trust is crucial. The Five Ambassadors framework[1] describes the behaviors of top-performing business people, particularly those in sales. It should be given careful consideration by sales and marketing management in the development of their plans since, ultimately, talented people are needed to ensure successful implementation.

Figure I. The Five Ambassadors framework

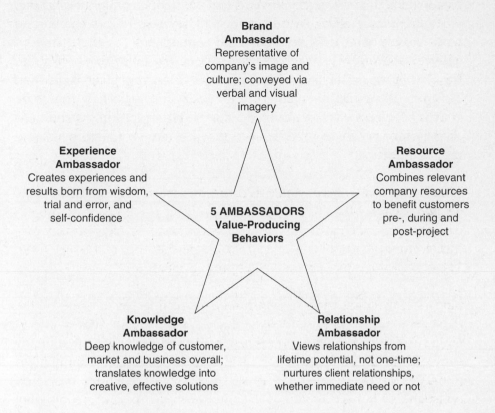

Brand Ambassador
Representative of company's image and culture; conveyed via verbal and visual imagery

Experience Ambassador
Creates experiences and results born from wisdom, trial and error, and self-confidence

5 AMBASSADORS Value-Producing Behaviors

Resource Ambassador
Combines relevant company resources to benefit customers pre-, during and post-project

Knowledge Ambassador
Deep knowledge of customer, market and business overall; translates knowledge into creative, effective solutions

Relationship Ambassador
Views relationships from lifetime potential, not one-time; nurtures client relationships, whether immediate need or not

The Five Ambassadors framework describes the behaviors of top performers. It has evolved over five years. Initially based on interviews with U.S. CEOs and top sales performers, it has been further developed since, through discussions with CEOs of companies in Asia and Europe, feedback from top sales performers in multiple industries, and student research of more than 90 companies in the United States and Asia since 2001.

Each of the Five Ambassadors is a specific behavior exhibited by the top performers at different times of their job. Typically, these behaviors were most prominent when the individual was selling a product, service or idea. The top performer shifted effortlessly from one Ambassador role to the next, depending on the specific business conditions they faced at that time. The Five Ambassadors behaviors were also exhibited when the top performers were seeking assistance (funding, budget increase, project help) from another party. These behaviors were rarely conscious. The top performer did not think to him or herself, "Now I must act like a resource ambassador." Rather, the Five Ambassadors were a fluid set of behaviors that ultimately convinced the other party of the merits of the argument being presented. Each of the Five Ambassadors encompassed multiple behaviors within itself, but the behaviors were sufficiently similar to be grouped into the broader Ambassador designations. Separately, each of the Five Ambassadors is an admirable set of behavior characteristics. Collectively, they are a powerful combination of skills that contributes to the overall success of the enterprise. Finally, the Five Ambassadors are not sequential behaviors. They are often simultaneous.

Brand Ambassador

This describes an individual's efforts to present their company, product or department to another person or group (customer, vendor or another internal department), using visual or verbal imagery. Visual imagery is self-explanatory: top performers are adept at using relevant visual examples to complement their presentation, making it memorable and connecting the audience to the initiative being presented. Verbal imagery deals with the words used to paint verbal pictures.

Resource Ambassador

Resource Ambassador describes the top performer's understanding of his or her own company. This is not merely a surface-level awareness of the company's products, but an in-depth understanding of its organization: the most influential people, how different departments contribute, and which resources would be most appealing and relevant to the buying or receiving party. It is often exhibited as an explicit description of which departments or functions were part of the solution being sold. For example, in the enterprise-software industry, a product sale is far more than just the software. It includes engineering support, customer service, warranties, consulting and more. Once the sale is made, the customer requires that the product works and functions as specified and, if not, wants to know what remedies are available. Top performers understand this and, in the pre-sales effort, work hard to describe these various resources to convince the customer that the company supports its products and to differentiate themselves from competing products. The bottom line is that the Resource Ambassador behaviors connect a company to the customer beyond the core product purchase by extending the product definition to include the areas that support it. As a result, the customer develops confidence that the company will support the products it sells.

Knowledge Ambassador

The Knowledge Ambassador encapsulates the knowledge that the top performer has and uses to describe for the buyer such things as market conditions, trends in the economic environment and similar information. The top performer presents this information throughout the sales or persuasion process to help the customer understand outside conditions and influences that could affect their business (explaining the "need" to buy the product). This information is gleaned from a wide range of sources (the Internet, magazines, newspapers) and becomes a crucial aspect of the top performer's efforts to win the customer. Top performers frequently update their market knowledge so that they can be an advocate for both the customer and their own company while demonstrating why the customer needs their products to be successful in the challenging environment described. The Knowledge Ambassador behaviors help the customer become smarter about their own business and understand why the seller's products are an integral piece of their success.

Relationship Ambassador

The Relationship Ambassador behaviors describe how sellers relate to buyers. A sales person must have a deep understanding of his or her buyers — not just the company overall, but the buyers individually, including who they are, what they like and dislike, what their interests are, what they have bought before and why they have bought it. The Relationship Ambassador behaviors continue even when a sale has been completed: the seller shifts to a more informal relationship, but always stays in contact. The seller wants to be the first person the buyer thinks of when it comes time to purchase again.

Experience Ambassador

The Experience Ambassador behaviors relate to the wisdom that comes from trial and error and the application of that wisdom every day.

Overall, the Five Ambassadors are a seamless pattern of behaviors exhibited by top performers. Rather than approaching each business relationship with a methodical, rigid plan outlining their behavior, the top performers combine spontaneity with thoughtful planning to achieve their objectives.

Sales managers understand the dual needs of quantitative and qualitative measures. The challenge is in determining what measures are most important so that a sales person's performance can be improved.

Companies have a significant investment in their sales forces and they want to see them succeed by producing a regular stream of sales from new and existing customers. Sales management must plan their sales activities each year based on corporate goals, market conditions and the performance expectations of each sales person. The challenges are sizable since markets, customers and competitors are constantly changing. The challenges are compounded by the relentless pressure to produce results. Sales management have to establish the right expectations via quotas and targets, monitor the activities of each sales person, keep the sales team focused on growing the business, motivate the team to keep working hard, and minimize interference from non-sales people in the organization.

But selling is also structured to be measured. Sales people are compensated based on whether and how they meet certain performance expectations. This book describes these objective measures. The Magic Numbers presented here help sales management assess the performance of their sales people beyond the normal activities such as number of calls made, focusing instead on more revealing measures.

There are 50 sales measures in this book, organized into three parts: Sales Planning; Sales Management and Selling; and Sales Performance and Review.

Part I: Sales Planning

The Magic Numbers in this section help sales management develop the sales plan, including understanding marketing conditions, forecasting opportunities, determining the ideal size of the sales force and setting price at the customer level.

Part II: Sales Management and Selling

The Magic Numbers in this section focus on two areas: compensation and customer. The compensation formulas help sales management determine and evaluate the rewards paid to sales people, and the customer measures offer insight into the financial quality of the customer relationship and the sales person's effectiveness with their customer base.

Part III: Sales Performance and Review

The Magic Numbers in this section help sales management evaluate the performance of sales people, comparing actual performance to plan.

Each measure is described using five categories:

1. The Definition
2. The Formula and Its Components
3. Where's the Data?
4. Calculating It
5. What It Means and Potential Challenges

Finally, while this book is designed as a reference for sales management and field sales representatives, marketers and senior management will also benefit from the measures described. The more that senior management, middle managers and employees understand about sales, the greater will be their understanding of the selling process, helping the entire organization appreciate more fully the vital role played by every company's sales people.

Endnote

[1] Davis, J. *Magic Numbers for Consumer Marketing,* John Wiley & Sons (Asia) Pte Ltd., 2005: pp. 116–128.

Part One

Magic Numbers for Sales Planning

Planning the sales effort requires an understanding of the market, forecasting, determining the sales-force size to meet goals, and working with marketing to influence price setting. Every sales effort begins with thoughtful planning to help sales professionals understand their market better and outline their activities. Strong market awareness enables the successful sales professional to determine more effectively how to structure the sales force to take advantage of company strengths and market opportunities.

Part One is thus organized into four main category areas: market assessment; forecasting; size of sales force; and factors to be considered when setting price.

Market Share

THE DEFINITION

Market share describes a company's sales (in units or dollars) as a percentage of total sales volume in a specific industry, market or product area.

THE FORMULA AND ITS COMPONENTS

It can be expressed with the following formula:

$$M_{it} = \frac{S_{it}}{\Sigma S_t}$$

Where

M_{it} = company i's market share in time t expressed in percentage terms
S_{it} = sales of company i in time t (in units or dollars)
ΣS_t = sum of all sales in time t (in units or dollars)

WHERE'S THE DATA?

Company sales figures are found in the accounting or finance departments. Sales figures for competitors in the same product market can be found in their annual reports (if they are publicly traded), in industry trade publications and business periodicals, and from market research reports and consulting firms. Once the measurement criteria have been identified (units or dollars; broad market or narrow geographic boundary;

and product definitions, for example), then gathering the relevant information is a matter of reviewing your own sales as compared to the sales of
the total market for similar products.

Sales and marketing managers should compare data from multiple
sources because of differences in data-collection time periods, reporting time periods, collection methodologies and the precision of measurement criteria.

CALCULATING IT

To illustrate, in 2004 Nike had $12.3 billion in sales out of total sales
of $33 billion[1] in the global athletic market. Thus, Nike's market share
was over 37%, calculated as follows:

$$\frac{\$12,300,000,000}{\$33,000,000,000} = 37.3\%$$

WHAT IT MEANS AND POTENTIAL CHALLENGES

Market share is typically used in several planning areas. As a business
planning metric, senior management may set a market-share target for
a forthcoming time period (typically one–two years) for the company.
Marketers use the Four Ps of the marketing mix (product, price, place,
promotion) to attract customers and develop a competitive advantage
for their company's products. Sales management would include the
market-share figures in their sales plans when discussing goals for the
upcoming business period. Market-share data serves as a goal for the sales
organization overall, for specific territories/offices, and for individual
performance objectives. Since sales people are in the field every day
working with customers and gaining insight into competitors' activities,
they have up-to-the-minute information on current market conditions
and any progress being made at the customer level. This information
should be shared with the rest of the company on a regular basis to
keep management up to date on the company's performance against
competitors and with customers.

A rising market share is generally a good sign, although it is subject
to several qualifications. The company's market share (in units) may

have risen because the company lowered its price substantially and may now be losing money. Or its share may have risen because the product category is aging and smarter firms are quickly abandoning the category, leaving the crumbs to this firm. Building on the athletic-market example, in 2005 Adidas announced its intention to acquire Reebok.[2] With this acquisition, Adidas would move closer to Nike's number-one market-share position. The Adidas-Reebok deal would have created a company with $11.1 billion in revenue in 2004, or nearly a 31% market share. Before the acquisition, Adidas' global market share was closer to 21–22%. Thus, Adidas' market-share increase is the result of acquisition, not necessarily a rising overall market, although that may be a possible contributor in the future.

Sales management need to analyze their market share in depth to gain a better understanding of the sources of their market-share performance. If market-share gains were made over a specified period of time, were they ahead of schedule or behind schedule? Is this increased share sustainable? If market share declined, what were the factors that may have caused this? Competitor innovation? Competitor pricing? Customer dissatisfaction? Changing customer preferences?

The key takeaway is that market share is a useful metric for both review and planning purposes.

Endnotes

[1] Adapted from two business reports: Hirsch, S and A. Tucker. "In a bid to step on Nike's toes, Adidas plans to buy Reebok". *The Baltimore Sun*, August 4, 2005; and Kang, S and M. Karnitschnig. "For Adidas, Reebok Deal Caps Push to Broaden Urban Appeal". *The Wall Street Journal*, August 4, 2005.
Estimates of the size of the total athletic-footwear market in 2004 varied between $33 billion and $35 billion. Assuming $35 billion, Nike's market share would be 35.1%.

[2] http://classwork.busadm.mu.edu/Giacomino/EMBA/NIKE%20article%209-20.04.html

Additional References

Davis, J. *Magic Numbers for Consumer Marketing*, John Wiley & Sons (Asia) Pte Ltd. 2005: pp. 30–34.
Davis, J. *Measuring Marketing: 103 Key Metrics Every Marketer Needs*, John Wiley & Sons (Asia) Pte Ltd., 2007.

2 Market Growth

THE DEFINITION

Market growth is defined as the percentage increase in sales (either in units or dollars) of an industry, market segment, or product category.

THE FORMULA AND ITS COMPONENTS

Market growth is determined by measuring the total sales in the market and then comparing this figure to the sales changes in preceding time periods (typically years). It is represented by the following formula:

$$G_m = \frac{R_I}{R_L}$$

Where

G_m = % market growth
R_I = dollars/units increase this year
R_L = dollars/units last year

WHERE'S THE DATA?

Market data can be easily obtained from industry trade publications, independent market-research firms, product analysts, reputable business magazines, government reports and trade associations.

CALCULATING IT

To illustrate using dollars, if the total revenues in the market are projected to be $500 million this year and were $400 million last year, then the market growth rate is 25%. This is calculated by dividing the revenue increase, $100 million, by total revenues last year, $400 million:

$$\frac{\$100 \text{ million}}{\$400 \text{ million}} = 0.25 \text{ or } 25\%$$

Using units, Sony sold 850,000 units of its Walkman digital music player in 2004. It forecast sales of 4.5 million units in 2005, for a projected growth rate of 529%. The market for portable digital music players was 37 million units in 2004 and was expected to be 57 million units in 2005, for a growth rate of 54%.[1] Knowing the market growth rate assists companies in determining whether their own performance is stronger, consistent with or weaker than the rest of the market.

Sony Digital Music Player Projected Growth

$$\frac{4,500,000 \text{ units}}{850,000 \text{ units}} = 5.29 \text{ or } 529\%$$

Digital Music Player Projected Market Growth

$$\frac{20 \text{ million units}}{37 \text{ million units}} = 0.54 \text{ or } 54\%$$

WHAT IT MEANS AND POTENTIAL CHALLENGES

Sales management are interested in growing the company's business in the territories in which it competes. Along with the marketing department, sales management are tasked with identifying growth opportunities along two dimensions: market share and financial performance. Growth has direct implications for a firm's competitive position. Company growth signals market acceptance of the firm's products (since customers are unlikely to adopt a new product if it does not satisfy their needs) and a potential competitive advantage (particularly if the growth is faster than that of competitors). Company management are keenly interested in whether company growth is faster, equal to, or less than market growth since the answer will affect future sales and marketing plans about customer segments, product choices, channels and even marketing communications programs.

Knowing the market growth rate can provide sales management with insight into the future potential for their business (although there is no guarantee that historical growth rates will continue into the future). A company's own growth must be measured first, for two reasons: first, to see what the growth trend has been over the past few years and to determine whether the current pace is above or below the recent historical average; and second, to compare its growth to that of the competition.

Market growth can serve as a good indicator of dynamics in the marketplace. It provides guidance on the market's potential (the total number of customers in the target market segment), the level of customer penetration (how many customers have entered the market) and the rate of customer entry (how quickly new customers enter the market).[2] As the Sony example indicates, the market growth rate can also suggest important trends, which can be further understood by comparing growth rates for the past four or five years and/or projected growth for the next few years. In Sony's case, its projected pace of growth far exceeds that of the overall market, which means Sony expects to gain market share, most likely at the expense of its rivals. Further analysis reveals that part of Sony's projection is influenced by the launch of new models of digital music player in 2005, probably with the hope that these new devices will capture the hearts and minds of consumers and eat into the market-leading position of its rival, Apple. Sales management and marketers will want to understand the forces driving this market growth and, in this instance, the reasons Sony's growth far exceeds the pace of the market. Demographic changes, purchase behavior patterns, product or market innovations and lower interest rates are examples of factors that may drive or influence the growth rate. Once the driving forces are understood, companies can use this information to develop new products, communications campaigns and price changes to create a competitive advantage for their products.

Market growth provides strategic guidance regarding the potential attractiveness of a given market in the years to come and assists marketing managers in understanding the associated opportunities and challenges. It is also a useful tool for senior management when evaluating marketing investments, since it provides a snapshot of likely growth opportunities. Venture capitalists, too, find market growth an important factor in evaluating the viability of start-up companies, since it can suggest whether a venture has a long-term future or not.

Developing a clear understanding of market growth is not complex, but it does require more effort than merely scanning the daily paper. Publicly traded companies produce annual reports for shareholders, containing detailed financial information and often providing insight into senior management's view of future opportunities. Whenever possible, sales management should provide first-hand insight from the field to marketing management, as this helps develop a more complete profile of market conditions. Marketers can and should avail themselves of this information as it will provide some general insight into their competition, albeit that annual reports rarely reveal detailed strategic choices. But because public companies have an obligation to report their performance to shareholders, a diligent marketer may succeed in gaining a clearer sense of the competitor's management style and will certainly be able to compare specific business performance to that of their own comparable products. Sales and marketing people working in private companies will benefit from their public-company competitor's annual reports as well. But to learn about other private companies and their respective strengths and weaknesses, marketers will need to conduct their own market research, hire a market research firm, or review industry trade publications for their sector.

The thoughtful reader will quickly note that the Sony example provides a frame of reference. In other words, Sony's projected 529% growth rate appears quite strong compared to the market overall. However, be aware that to measure growth, a marketer must be quite clear about what is being measured and why. Is it growth of total market revenues? Or growth of total market dollars available for purchasing? Or is it the rate at which new customers are being acquired? Or the rate at which the three-to-five most significant competitors are growing? The answer depends on the industry. Furthermore, even within industries there are segments that may perform far differently from others.

Endnotes

[1] Hall, K. "Can Sony's New Walkman Run?" *BusinessWeek Online*, September 9, 2005.

[2] Best, R. J. *Market-Based Management: Strategies for Growing Customer Value and Profitability*, Pearson Education, 2005: pp. 72, 73.

Additional References

Davis, J. *Magic Numbers for Consumer Marketing*, John Wiley & Sons (Asia) Pte Ltd. 2005: pp. 18–22.

Davis, J. *Measuring Marketing: 103 Key Metrics Every Marketer Needs*, John Wiley & Sons (Asia) Pte Ltd., 2007.

3

Market Penetration

THE DEFINITION

Market penetration is a comparison of current market demand and potential market demand for a company's products. Sales representatives are responsible for developing successful and profitable relationships with customers, and market penetration is one of four strategies sales management can employ to improve their success with customers and increase market share as a result.

THE FORMULA AND ITS COMPONENTS[1]

The formula is as follows:

$$M_P = \frac{D_c}{D_p} \times 100$$

Where

M_P = market penetration
D_c = current market demand
D_p = potential market demand

WHERE'S THE DATA?

To conduct any sales and marketing analysis properly, it is important to use more than one source. Each source may employ a different research methodology, including subtle differences in survey questions, for example, that yield widely different results.

Sales management of publicly traded firms can find the information in annual reports. Sales people from privately held companies will have to talk to their accounting and finance team to get the numbers, or at least the overall rate of growth, in order to compare their performance to that of the rest of the market.

Market data can be easily obtained from industry trade publications, independent market-research firms, product analysts, reputable business magazines, government reports and trade associations.

Sales figures for competitors can be found in their annual reports, if they are publicly traded, or possibly in industry trade publications or market-research reports. Surveys conducted either in-house or by outside market-research firms can provide valuable data as well.

CALCULATING IT

"Current market demand" describes the total number of products that could be purchased by a pre-defined target group in a specific market area under specific business conditions and marketing programs for all firms in the market.

"Potential market demand" describes the *added* opportunities available to the same companies for the same products under the same conditions. Potential market demand is influenced by type of product, pricing, new marketing appeals and competitors' actions. Some products lend themselves to added potential, such as many consumer non-durables (food, beverage and grocery products, for example), while other products have less added potential, such as a sports or entertainment events. This is due partly to the types of products (when popular grocery items are discounted, for instance, it often drives temporary demand and increases the total dollars in the market than would otherwise have "naturally" been spent). Sports and entertainment events have a narrower appeal (everyone needs food, not everyone needs to see a professional soccer match) and limited live seating. Additional marketing spent on these will generate increased costs per remaining seat.

Market penetration is effectively a method for measuring potential opportunities for the market overall. A corollary measure in this evaluation is known as the "market-share index", a particularly useful measure for individual companies. Market-share index helps sales and marketing management determine which areas of their operation need adjustment to improve market penetration. It is closely related to market share, providing more specific information about the factors that influence customers' purchase decisions and, ultimately, market share.

The formula for measuring market-share index is as follows:[2]

$$M_{si} = P_a \times P_P \times B_i \times A \times P_{pur}$$

Where

M_{si} = market-share index

P_a = product awareness (The number of people aware of the product in the target market compared to the overall population in the target market)

P_p = product preference (Is the product and/or its features attractive?)

B_i = intention to buy (Is the product's price attractive?)

A = availability of product (Can the product be found in the marketplace?)

P_{pur} = product purchase (Is buying the product a positive experience?)

Using the first formula for market penetration, let's assume we are analyzing the market for a new canned food in a selected city. The market is highly fragmented, meaning multiple competitors are vying for market share, but no single competitor dominates. Current demand indicates a market totaling $8 million in sales annually. However, past industry sales and marketing efforts indicate that price promotions boost business by 25%. Therefore, the market potential is $10,000,000 ($8,000,000 × 0.25 = $2,000,000. This result is added to the $8,000,000 current demand to determine potential demand). Therefore,

$$M_P = \frac{\$8,000,000}{\$10,000,000} \times 100$$

$$= 80\%$$

The result shows a market penetration of 80%. For most markets, this result would be quite high, suggesting that acquiring the remaining customer potential would be increasingly expensive on a per-customer basis. However, let's assume that, based on current market dynamics, a sales promotion at this time will lead to business increases of 75%. Therefore, the market potential is $14,000,000 ($8,000,000 × 0.75 = $6,000,000. This result is added to the $8,000,000 current demand to determine potential demand), as follows:

$$M_P = \frac{\$8,000,000}{\$14,000,000} \times 100$$

$$= 57\%$$

Market penetration is now 57%, which suggests that there is more room for all canned-food companies in the market to improve their growth potential. The market penetration calculations describe the market overall.

Now let's look at growth opportunities for individual companies in this highly fragmented market. Using the second formula for market-share index, let's assume that a canned-food company's data gathering reveals the following statistics for their business:

- P_a = product awareness = 52% (48% are unaware)

- P_p = product preference = 76% (24% find it unattractive)

- B_i = intention to buy = 55% (45% do not intend to buy)

- A = availability of product = 40% (60% product not available)

- P_{pur} = product purchase = 38% (62% had a disappointing purchase experience)

Plugging these figures into the formula reveals that our canned-food firm has a market-share index of 3.3%, as follows:

$$M_{si} = P_a \times P_p \times B_i \times A \times P_{pur}$$
$$M_{si} = 0.52 \times 0.76 \times 0.55 \times 0.40 \times 0.38$$

$$= 0.033$$

$$= 3.3\%$$

Sales and marketing management now have data indicating that the overall market is only 57% penetrated by all competitors and that their own share is 3.3%. Therefore, with the right mix of promotions and selling techniques, their market share can improve, perhaps dramatically.

Had the market penetration rate been closer to 100%, the task of improving share would have been significantly harder, since all companies are vying for a limited set of remaining customers.

A helpful framework when conducting market-penetration analysis is the Ansoff Matrix, conceived by Igor Ansoff in his 1957 *Harvard Business Review* article "Strategies for Diversification".[3] Ansoff describes growth opportunities in a simple two-by-two matrix, with products across the horizontal axis and markets along the vertical axis, as shown below:

Figure 3.1   The Ansoff Matrix

PRODUCTS

		Present	New
MARKETS	**Present**	Market Penetration	Product Development
	New	Market Development	Diversification

The Ansoff Matrix is a useful supplement in determining market penetration because it provides clear guidance on the sales and marketing growth choices: growth opportunities are limited to existing products in existing markets. This prescribes a set of activities available to sales and marketing managers in order to penetrate existing markets successfully. The activities are:

- Increase market share in the existing market — companies are attracting customers within the segment who are either buying competing products or who fit the target profile but have not yet committed. Sales and marketing management can influence this through different sales techniques and volume price programs, more advertising, short-term promotions or, most expensively (although potentially the most productive over the long term), increased customer-relationship development. This is the competitive situation commonly associated with many branded consumer products with similar or identical ingredients but frequently updated marketing messages. The challenge is the expense of improving sales techniques and regularly creating fresh, relevant marketing campaigns that resonate with consumers.

- First-mover advantage — also known as "securing dominant share". Usually, the sales representative is selling an innovative product that attracts the market's attention before the competition has a chance to enter, allowing the firm to capture a dominant market share. However, securing a long-term majority share is very difficult without substantial investment in the continuous building of customer relationships, marketing and R&D (the latter also begins to shift the company from a growth strategy built around market penetration to one that emphasizes product development). Technology markets, including software and consumer electronics, often have this approach. The challenge here lies in sustaining the advantage beyond the short term.

- Deep price penetration — this is an aggressive, low-price-point strategy designed to steal share aggressively from competitors by undercutting them on price. A classic example was seen in the United States in the 1980s, when Japanese chip manufacturers flooded the market with below-cost chips to gain market share. The challenges in such a strategy are in determining the break-even point and raising prices later on, as customers adopt the offerings and the company seeks to improve profitability.

- Increase product usage by current customers — this can be done by developing new uses for the product or creating customer-loyalty plans. Examples of this can be found in the airline and hotel industries. The attendant challenges are the cost of maintaining up-to-date information on customers (often through expensive software systems and databases), the cost of accumulated points programs or frequent-flyer miles redeemed within a short period of time, and the cost of finding new personalized sales and marketing approaches that continue to reinforce the importance the company places on the relationship.

WHAT IT MEANS AND POTENTIAL CHALLENGES

Market penetration helps companies assess remaining growth potential. The market-share index analysis indicates where firms may have problems in their "go to market" efforts, highlighting those areas that can help improve penetration. For example, in the above analysis, 76% of the people who are aware of the canned-food company's product prefer it, which is a reasonably strong level of preference for the product. Interestingly, only 52% of the market is aware of the product. Therefore, the company can focus its sales efforts on deeper customer relationships and its marketing efforts on communications to increase awareness. If, through these efforts, this company succeeds in increasing awareness to 75%, then its market-share index increases from 3.3% to 4.7%, as shown below.

$$M_{si} = 0.75 \times 0.76 \times 0.55 \times 0.40 \times 0.38$$
$$= 0.047$$
$$= 4.7\%$$

In this example, another area of improvement is in the buying experience. Only 38% of the buyers had a good buying experience. Therefore, the company could undertake a point-of-sale training program that teaches sales and customer-service employees how to improve service with a view to enhancing their customers' purchasing experience. Let's assume the company is able to flip these numbers through just such a training program, so that 62% of the buyers report a positive buying experience. Keeping the aforementioned increase in awareness level and now factoring in the improved buying experience yields a market penetration of 7.8%, as follows:

$$M_{si} = 0.75 \times 0.76 \times 0.55 \times 0.40 \times 0.62$$
$$= 0.078$$
$$= 7.8\%$$

Be aware that understanding each variable in the market-share index has its own challenges. Product awareness is a percentage measure of customers in the target market that are aware of a company's products (the percentage of people overall in the market that are aware of the product could be measured, but this would be less meaningful because it would presume that all people in the market may have an interest in the product if they were only aware of it). If awareness is low, then this result indicates that the company has the potential to increase awareness. The corollary is that it will cost money to increase awareness since marketing will have to invest in advertising, sales promotions and other marketing communications efforts. Improving the buyer's satisfaction at the time of purchase will also cost money. But if the company's goal is to improve penetration and beat the competition, then these are worthy of serious consideration.

As the Ansoff Matrix indicates, decision making for market penetration is clear cut since sales and marketing management are concerned only with known products and known markets. While the investment in marketing plans (pricing and advertising, in particular) and sales programs (promotions and volume selling) can be heavy, it is unlikely to involve much market research or R&D, since both of those would shift the company's strategy to different growth quadrants and, correspondingly, different marketing and product approaches. Firms focusing on market penetration may have a unique relationship with customers, developed over many years or even decades of tradition, thus minimizing the need to seek growth elsewhere. It is a unique and conservative business approach, but if a company is too successful, it is only a matter of time before competitors enter, forcing the company to consider a response from the other quadrants.

To determine potential market demand, sales management must push marketers to conduct and analyze customer research, evaluate trends, establish product pricing, determine distribution, and create promotional campaigns to generate awareness. Sales management then work directly with customers, developing relationships, understanding customer profiles and determining specific solutions to address customers' needs. Once a customer base is established, the challenge is how to continue growing this increasingly valuable asset.

Endnotes

[1] Kotler, P., M. L. Siew, H. A. Swee and C. T. Tan. *Marketing Management: An Asian Perspective*, Prentice Hall, 2003: p. 137.

[2] Best, R. J. *Market-Based Management: Strategies for Growing Customer Value and Profitability*, Pearson Education, 2005: pp. 72, 86–87

[3] Ansoff, H. I. "Strategies for Diversification", *Harvard Business Review*, 35(2), September–October (1957).

Additional References

Davis, J., *Magic Numbers for Consumer Marketing*, John Wiley & Sons (Asia) Pte Ltd. 2005: pp. 34–36.

Davis, J. *Measuring Marketing: 103 Key Metrics Every Marketer Needs*, John Wiley & Sons (Asia) Pte Ltd., 2007.

MAGIC
NUM8ER
4

Market Demand

THE DEFINITION

Market demand describes the total demand for a particular product and/or service from new and existing customers. Magic Numbers 1 and 2 described market share and market growth, which are both key measures in a sales and marketing performance assessment "toolbox". Sales and marketing management need to measure total demand since it helps them understand potential growth opportunities.

THE FORMULA AND ITS COMPONENTS[1]

This is the sum of existing/repeat customers plus new customers, and it can be used to measure company-level or market-level demand. It is represented by the formula:

$$M_{dt} = P_{rt} + P_{nt}$$

Where

M_{dt} = market demand during time period t
P_{rt} = repeat or replacement purchases in time period t (in dollars)
P_{nt} = new purchases in time period t (in dollars)

WHERE'S THE DATA?

At the market level, data for demand, repeat purchases and new purchases can be found in industry trade journals and research reports, general business magazines with special issues devoted to specific industry sectors, and the marketer's own research into market trends. At the firm level, marketers will have to rely on a combination of their own internal reports for information on current and new customers as well as market research to gauge market demand.

CALCULATING IT

Let's assume that a Southeast Asian dried-foods manufacturing business sells its products direct to retailers. Last year, purchases from their existing/repeat retail customers totaled $5 million, while purchases from new customers amounted to $2 million. Market demand for their product is, therefore, $7 million.

$5,000,000 + $2,000,000 = $7,000,000

WHAT IT MEANS AND POTENTIAL CHALLENGES

Market demand helps marketers understand the sources of customer demand for their products and/or services. It provides basic insight into their target customer base and can be an early indicator of the effectiveness of marketing and sales programs. An increasing demand from new customers is generally considered a positive signal that the market is growing and wants more of the product. A decline in existing customers may be cause for concern, suggesting that competitors are offering better products, lower prices or a combination of both. However, it would be wise to investigate the market more deeply before reaching conclusions from market-demand data alone.

Market demand is particularly useful for marketers when discussing their target customers in planning meetings with senior management and in the written marketing plan itself. For this to be measured properly, a marketer must have a clear and empirically based explanation of the new and existing customer figures used. Otherwise, the market-demand figure will be purely an exercise in guessing, which will harm the marketer's ability to defend the rest of the marketing plan convincingly.

Market demand is an important planning metric, particularly when used in combination with market growth, since an increase in both measures may indicate that a company is taking thoughtful advantage of a rising market in both retaining existing customers and capturing new ones. Furthermore, market demand can be a useful starting point for establishing sales objectives at both the strategic and tactical levels. Strategic sales objectives include revenue targets at the market and segment levels. Tactical sales objectives would focus on more detailed expectations at the individual customer-account level. A clear understanding of market demand will therefore help sales management establish appropriate sales quotas for their field sales personnel. This will be discussed at greater length in the sections on customers and sales force quotas.

Endnote

[1] Best, R. J. *Market-Based Management: Strategies for Growing Customer Value and Profitability*, Pearson Education, 2005: p. 77.

Additional References

Davis, J. *Magic Numbers for Consumer Marketing*, John Wiley & Sons (Asia) Pte Ltd. 2005: pp. 46–47.

Davis, J. *Measuring Marketing: 103 Key Metrics Every Marketer Needs*, John Wiley & Sons (Asia) Pte Ltd., 2007.

Doyle, C. *Collins Internet-Linked Dictionary of Marketing*, Harper Collins, 2003, 2006: p. 177.

5 Causal Forecast

THE DEFINITION

Causal forecasts help companies determine future performance based on external factors, or causes.

THE FORMULA AND ITS COMPONENTS

A commonly used technique in causal forecasting is linear regression. In the linear regression method, when the dependent variable (usually the vertical axis on a graph) changes as a result of the change in another variable (plotted as the horizontal axis), it reflects a causal relationship and is represented by a straight line drawn through closely related data points on a graph with an x and y axis. Simply put, linear regression is used to determine if there is a trend to the data, and is represented by a line formula:

$$y = a + bx$$

Where

y = the dependent variable
a = the intercept
b = the slope of the line
x = the independent variable

As can be surmised, to determine the line formula both the slope of the line, designated as "b" above, and the intercept, designated as "a", must be calculated. The reason for this is that the slope describes the effect of the independent variable, x, on the dependent variable, y (i.e. the changes in y if x changes by one unit). If there is no relationship between the dependent and independent variables, then the slope of the line would equal zero. The intercept describes where the linear regression line intersects with the y axis. The formulas are:

Intercept = a = Y − bX

$$\text{Slope} \quad = b = \frac{\sum xy - nXY}{\sum x^2 - nX^2}$$

Where

a = intercept
b = slope of the line
X = $\sum$x = mean of x
n = the x data
Y = $\sum$y = mean of y
n = the y data
n = number of periods

From here, the strength of the relationship between the dependent and independent variable must be measured. This is known as "correlation" and is represented by:

$$r = \frac{n\sum xy - \sum x \sum y}{\sqrt{[n\sum x^2 - (\sum x)^2][n\sum y^2 - (\sum y)^2]}}$$

Where

r = correlation coefficient
n = number of periods
x = the independent variable
y = the dependent variable

Finally, forecasters need to calculate the percentage of variation in the dependent (y) variable that is attributed to the independent (x) variable. The coefficient of determination is used (which measures the relationship between the dependant and independent variables). If the independent variable is changed, then what effect does that have on the dependent variable? Do the two variables "go together"? The closer the relationship, the larger the coefficient of determination, up to 1.0 (or –1.0 for negative relationships). It is calculated by:

$$r = r^2$$

WHERE'S THE DATA?

External business data for causal forecasts typically comes from published demographic information from industry research reports and trade journals. This information includes:

- Population trends
- Taxes (corporate, income and/or retail sales taxes)
- Pricing data
- License fees
- Income levels.

The outside factors that can influence a company's projections extend beyond these. The data is often lumped into the following four categories:

- Political influences (law, regulations, legal)
- Economic (interest rates, money supply, market share, customer growth trends)
- Social (current culturally acceptable practices, behaviors and activities)
- Technological (innovations that change cost conditions, supply chains and labor needs).

Company forecasts do differ as each senior management team evaluates external factors differently; so reviewing common outside influences from industry reports may not offer management enough detail for their own forecasting purposes. However, company management should determine criteria they believe are most relevant to their common and typical business conditions. Once the criteria are established, each annual forecasting exercise can then focus on the specific data required to make a decision that is consistent with company criteria. The criteria should also be revisited every year to ensure relevance, particularly since business and economic conditions are not static and changes happen quickly.

Internal data that guide forecasting will come from a combination of performances in recent time periods (with emphasis placed on more recent periods) and management's interpretation of their growth needs and the company's ability to perform beyond expectations (either internal, industry or investor expectations).

CALCULATING IT

Let's use an example to illustrate how these various formulas work together.

- Restaurant Steak House
- Forecasting food sales
  - How many meals will be sold each week
- Forecasting Inventory
  - Perishable food
  - Non-perishable food

Figure 5.1   Causal forecast for Steak House

Week	# of meals served	Quantity of beef ordered (lbs)			
	X	Y	XY	X^2	Y^2
1	100	125	12,500	10,000	15,625
2	150	186	27,900	22,500	34,596
3	90	125	11,250	8,100	15,625
4	125	142	17,750	15,625	20,164
5	130	150	19,500	16,900	22,500
6	120	135	16,200	14,400	18,225
7	115	140	16,100	13,225	19,600
8	75	96	7,200	5,625	9,216
9	100	130	13,000	10,000	16,900
10	105	133	13,965	11,025	17,689
TOTAL	1,110	1,362	155,365	127,400	190,140

A linear regression is then calculated as follows:

X = 1,110/10 = 111

Y = 1,362/10 = 136.20

$$b = \frac{\sum xy - nXY}{\sum x^2 - nX^2} = \frac{(155,365) - (10)\,(111)\,(136.20)}{(127,400) - (10)\,(111)^2}$$

b = 0.9983

a = Y − bX = 136.20 − 0.9983(111)

a = 25.3887

These results are plugged into the original line formula:

$y = a + bx$

y = 25.3887 + 0.9983(x)

For "x", the forecaster should select the number of meals to be served (using this example) to calculate "y". Let's select 130, as that is the approximate average number of meals served per day:

y = 25.3887 + 0.9983(130)

y = 155.17

Therefore, 155 pounds of beef should be ordered.

Next, the correlation coefficient is calculated to determine the strength of the relationship (also known as "interdependence") between x and y.

$$r = \frac{n\sum xy - \sum x\sum y}{\sqrt{[n\sum x^2 - (\sum x)^2][n\sum y^2 - (\sum y)^2]}}$$

$$r = \frac{10(155,365) - (1,110)(1,362)}{\sqrt{[10(127,400) - (1,110)^2][10(190,140) - (1,363)^2]}}$$

r = 0.9783

$r^2 = 0.9571$

The results suggest there is a strong relationship between the number of meals served and the quantity (in lbs.) of beef ordered. This restaurant can therefore feel confident that its forecast will be accurate.

WHAT IT MEANS AND POTENTIAL CHALLENGES

Causal forecasts help managers measure the relationship between two types of variables: dependent and independent. Managers may seek to understand how much product (the dependent variable, or the "output") should be ordered under given demand conditions (the independent variable, or the "input"). As demand conditions change, so too should the amount of product ordered. The value (size, quantity, amount) of the dependent variable is directly influenced by the independent variable. Thus, a change in a product or marketing program can affect buyers' behaviors (a price reduction might lead to increased purchases). Or an emerging trend may signal greater opportunity for existing or new products, changing the performance of the business as a result. Causal forecasting enables managers to measure the possible impact to their business (and/or customers or other value-chain participants) from these changes.

For example, companies such as Nike or Adidas, both of which make athletic footwear, would be interested in forecasting how many basketball shoes they may sell to teen basketball players in the United States over the next three years. By reviewing census data of the teen population and surveys of growth trends in teen basketball, they can project the potential demand for their respective products. Assuming the teen population is forecast to grow (the independent variable), as is the interest in basketball, then it is plausible to project an increase in sales (the dependent variable).

Other examples might include:

- Demand increases for air conditioners during summer months
- Increases/decreases in ice cream sales due to temperature changes
- More workers needed at restaurants on busy nights.

With regard to the linear regression example used above, the result suggests that the costs of the product can be predicted fairly accurately.

By extension, the final price offered to the customer can even be determined as well. Marketers in this example will want to set prices based on their strategic objectives for the positioning of their restaurant, its image (premium, mass market, value), cost factors and the projected amount of business in the future.

For sales people, causal forecasts are useful, particularly with controllable activities such as short-term promotions, where the outcome can be reasonably anticipated.

Causal forecasting is not useful in every situation. It works best when the correlation between the dependent and independent variables is strong.

References

Davis, J. *Measuring Marketing: 103 Key Metrics Every Marketer Needs*, John Wiley & Sons (Asia) Pte Ltd., 2007.

Lapide, L. "New Developments in Business Forecasting", *Journal of Business Forecasting Methods & Systems*, Vol. 18, Issue 2 (Summer 1999).

http://morris.wharton.upenn.edu/forecast, *Principles of Forecasting, A Handbook for Researchers and Practitioners*, Edited by J. Scott Armstrong, University of Pennsylvania.

www.uoguelph.ca/~dsparlin/forecast.htm. Cachon, G. and C. Terwiesch, *Matching Supply with Demand: An Introduction to Operations Management*, International edition, McGraw-Hill, 2006.

6

Time-Series Analysis

THE DEFINITION

Time-series analysis is a forecasting technique used to evaluate data to determine patterns and trends. The findings can help company management determine the best market opportunities to exploit.

THE FORMULAS AND THEIR COMPONENTS

Time-series analysis is a useful method for using past quantitative data to predict future performance. Three popular methods are:

- Naïve forecast

- Averaging forecasts

- Exponential smoothing.

Each method uses demand from previous period(s) as the key variable. A combination of formulas and/or charts is used to illustrate each method.

WHERE'S THE DATA?

Demand data is found in company annual reports. For publicly traded firms, the reports are published and the general data is accessible through the "investors sections" on company websites. Privately held companies will keep the data in their accounting and/or finance departments. In either case, the company data may be presented in aggregate so that individual customer segments and product lines are not clearly delineated. To acquire meaningful data for time-series forecasting purposes, sales management will need to talk directly to their finance and accounting counterparts to specify the detail being sought to ensure forecasts are for the right markets using the right data.

CALCULATING IT[1]

Naïve forecast

The naïve forecast assumes the next period's demand will match that of the previous period. It is important that the selected forecast quantity is consistent in both the actual and forecast columns (i.e. use dollars in both, or units). Naïve forecasts are more clearly explained with a simple chart, rather than a formula.

Figure 6.1   Naïve forecast chart

Period	Actual Sales (dollars)	Forecast Sales (dollars)
January	75	
February	75	75
March	90	75
April	110	90
May	120	110
June	120	120
July	150	120
August	110	150
September	100	110
October	90	100
November	100	90
December	130	100

Averaging forecasts

Averaging forecasts have several approaches. Moving averages and weighted moving averages are two of the most common approaches.

* Moving average

Forecasters would select a representative number of periods and calculate the average of those periods. The result becomes the forecast amount for the next period. Let's assume a four-month forecast period using the previous chart. In this case, the forecast would represent the total sales in the January–April timeframe divided by the number of periods (four), to arrive at May's moving average. As the chart illustrates, May's forecast sales are 88. The same process is repeated to determine June's forecast sales (99), July's (110), and so on.

Figure 6.2   Moving average forecast chart

Period	Actual Sales (000s dollars)	Forecast Sales (000s dollars)
January	75	
February	75	
March	90	
April	110	
May	120	88
June	120	99
July	150	110
August	110	125
September	100	125
October	90	120
November	100	113
December	130	103

The moving average forecast helps correct the simplistic assumptions of the naïve forecast since it is likely that the previous period's sales are not perfectly repeatable in the next period. Moving average helps smooth over variations attributable to seasonal patterns. The moving average of sales performance based on the preceding three months (in this example) reduces the chance that any one month's exceptional performance (good or bad) will unduly influence the next month's forecast. However, more recent sales data is usually considered more reliable than older data since it may be indicative of current market conditions. Moving average forecasts do not account for this since the impact of recent data is reduced by the inclusion of older data in the average. The weighted moving average can help overcome this bias.

• Weighted moving average

The weighted moving average (or "simple" weighted average) assigns weights to data in different periods with, generally speaking, more recent periods receiving a higher weighting because they are considered more influential. The sum total of all the weights equals one; therefore, each weight is a fraction of one. Let's continue with the same example, assigning the lowest weight to the earliest month and the highest weight to the most recent as follows: 0.1, 0.2, 0.3, 0.4:

May = January (75*0.1) + February (75*0.2) + March (90*0.3) + April (110*0.4) = 93.5

June = February (75*0.1) + March (90*0.2) + April (110*0.3) + May (120*0.4) = 106.5

July = March (90*0.1) + April (110*0.2) + May (120*0.3) + June (120*0.4) = 115

August = April (110*0.1) + May (120*0.2) + June (120*0.3) + July (150*0.4) = 131

September = May (120*0.1) + June (120*0.2) + July (150*0.3) + August (110*0.4) = 125

October = June (120*0.1) + July (150*0.2) + August (110*0.3) + September (100*0.4) = 115

November = July (150*0.1) + August (110*0.2) + September (110*0.3) + October (90*0.4) = 106

December = August (110*0.1) + September (100*0.2) + October (90*0.3) + November (100*0.4) = 98

Figure 6.3   Weighted moving average forecast

Period	Actual Sales (000s dollars)	Forecast Sales (000s dollars)
January	75	
February	75	
March	90	
April	110	
May	120	93.5
June	120	106.5
July	150	115
August	110	131
September	100	125
October	90	115
November	100	106
December	130	98

Exponential smoothing[1]

Exponential smoothing is a more sophisticated approach to weighted moving average. It, too, is a popular forecasting technique used in computerized forecasting programs and wholesale and retail inventory ordering programs. Like the weighted moving average, exponential smoothing favors more recent data over older data. A key difference, however, is the use of a "smoothing constant" called alpha, represented by α. Alpha describes the level of smoothing deemed reasonable and the speed of a company's reaction to differences between forecasts and actual occurrences. As with weighted moving average, smoothing is a technique for reducing the impact of seasonality or more extreme variances from typical demand performance. It is always less than one and is based on the marketing forecaster's intuition of what comprises a good response rate combined with the nature of the product itself.

$$F_t = F_{t-1} + \alpha(A_t - F_{t-1})$$

Where

F_t = new forecast
A_t = actual demand that occurred in the forecast period
F_{t-1} = previous/most recent forecast

Forecasters begin the analysis with a previous period, building sequentially to arrive at the forecast for the period needed. This requires the forecaster to have past data and/or the initial forecast from which to develop the analysis. Adapting the earlier table, let's develop a forecast for April. To determine this, the forecasts for February and March must be calculated. For February, we need to know F_{t-1}, the previous/most recent forecast (January, in this case). Let's assume it was 70 and that alpha is 0.6. The following result occurs for February:

$$F_t = 70 + 0.6(75 - 70) = 73$$

An identical approach is used to determine the figures for March:

$$F_t = 73 + 0.6(75 - 73) = 74.2$$

Finally, April is then calculated:

$$F_t = 74.20 + 0.6(90 - 74.20) = 83.68$$

Figure 6.4   Exponential smoothing

Period	Actual Sales (000s dollars)	Forecast Sales (000s dollars)
January	75	70
February	75	73
March	90	74.20
April		83.68
May		
June		
July		
August		
September		
October		
November		
December		

Once the actual data for April is known, May can then be forecast, and the process continues as each month's actual sales are included.

WHAT IT MEANS AND POTENTIAL CHALLENGES

Marketers must regularly make decisions about future marketing activities. Strategic alignment with overall corporate objectives, marketing program investments and budgets, pricing, and customer development are among the many activities included in the typical marketing manager's responsibilities. These activities are part of the overall marketing planning effort and many of the marketing planning decisions are based on forecasting future sales. Understanding past sales performance is helpful in this regard as historical results often reveal trends that, depending on anticipated business conditions, influence the marketing plan recommendations.

Marketing managers have the responsibility to develop forecasts that help their companies determine demand for products and services. A thoughtful time-series forecast utilizes historical data (otherwise they are unreliable guesses). It serves as a starting guide for forecasting your company's possible future(s), from which your marketing recommendations logically flow. It helps marketers observe and understand seasonal variation patterns in data as well as any growth rate changes. However, marketers must be alert to the pros and cons of time-series forecasts:

- They are never 100% reliable.

- Time-series forecasts tend to be more accurate with shorter time frames (i.e. it is easier to predict tomorrow than it is next month, or next year).

- Time-series analysis tends to assume that the future will be like the past.

- Time-series forecasts tend to be more credible when based on longer data histories (i.e. using several months or years of data is better than several days).

- Newer data tend to be more reliable than older data and receive a higher weighting as a result.

Marketers must ask themselves a key question when considering forecasting needs: Is sales trend increasing, decreasing, flat? Time-series analysis can be helpful in answering basic trend questions as it may suggest emerging opportunities or, conversely, warning signs. But it is less useful for understanding and determining the causes that underlie trends. How do anomalous events such as external market disturbances (natural or man-made disasters), aggressive new marketing campaigns or competitive behavior affect demand? What are the reasons for the seasonal variation? Time-series analysis is a good first step toward developing a better forecast, but marketers must consider these other influences when developing their marketing plans.

Endnotes

[1] Adapted from http://www.referenceforbusiness.com/management/Ex-Gov/Forecasting.html

[2] Cachon, G. and C. Terwiesch. *Matching Supply with Demand: An Introduction to Operations Management*, International edition, McGraw-Hill, 2006.

Additional References

Davis, J. *Measuring Marketing: 103 Key Metrics Every Marketer Needs*, John Wiley & Sons (Asia) Pte Ltd., 2007.

Doyle, C. *Collins Internet-Linked Dictionary of Marketing*, Harper Collins, 2003, 2006: p. 296.

Imber, J. and B. A. Toffler. *Dictionary of Marketing Terms*, Barron's Educational Series, 2000: p. 545.

http://www.bized.ac.uk/timeweb/crunching/crunch_analysis_illus.htm

http://home.ubalt.edu/ntsbarsh/stat-data/Forecast.htm#rgintroduction

http://gbr.pepperdine.edu/001/forecast.html

http://www.tutor2u.net/business/marketing/sales_forecasting.asp

Independent Sales Representative Analysis

THE DEFINITION

Sales management have three basic choices when building their sales force: 100% company-employed sales people, an independent sales force, or a combination of these two. Independent sales reps are not employees of the company; they are non-company sales experts who are contracted to perform field sales activities that include prospecting for qualified customers, negotiating with them and closing deals.

A critical need is determining whether to have a company-owned sales force and the associated higher fixed costs, or an independent sales force. Sales managers then need to compare these two approaches to determine the most cost-effective approach for their company. An analysis of independent sales representatives is used to evaluate their financial attractiveness to the company.

THE FORMULA AND ITS COMPONENTS[1]

The analysis begins with setting the cost of a company sales force and an independent sales force equal to each other:

cost of company sales force = cost of independent sales force

Sales management would need to determine the break-even level of sales, below which the independent sales force would be more attractive and above which the dedicated sales force is the more sensible approach. To do this, cost comparisons need to be made.

WHERE'S THE DATA

The data for company-employed sales people will come from one or more of the following sources:

- The company's existing compensation data for any current or recent sales representatives. The human resources (personnel) department will have this information. Sales management, of course, should have a complete compensation profile of its current or recent sales representatives.

- Industry-specific reports of compensation levels for sales people in the industry and/or geographical area. These can be commissioned either to an independent consulting company or a market-research firm.

- Trade publications for the specific industry. Trade publications often research business trends in their industry, including recent compensation levels.

- Competitors' sales representatives interviewing for a job at the company.

- Trade shows and conferences. Sales management can and should use such events to learn about compensation practices, competitors' offerings and meet potential new customers.

The data for independent sales representatives will come from any of the following sources:

- Industry-specific listings of independent sales agent firms. These are usually published in industry trade publications. Sales management should review the various firms and their company information, including meeting with their management, to determine if there is a good fit between the two companies.

- Reputation and word of mouth. Sales management should regularly network with professionals in their industry to learn the latest trends and rumors. This informal information source is often invaluable. Of course, seasoned professionals will also want to evaluate any informal information they learn against their own instincts and with comparisons to those they trust in the industry.

- An independent consulting or a market-research firm; or published industry data such as that shown in the tables opposite.

CALCULATING IT

The tables below reflect the salaries for 2001 of customer-service representations in the insurance industry in the United States, in rural and urban locations.[2]

Figure 7.1   2001 Rural agency service rep salary ranges

POSITION	SALARY RANGE
Personal CSR 2+ years	$21,329-$25,220
Personal CSR Under 2 years	$17,726-$19,358
Commercial CSR 7+ years	$27,919-$32,431
Commercial CSR 2 to 7 years	$20,791-$23,518
Commercial CSR Under 2 years	$18,686-$20,686
Employee Benefits CSR	$22,450-$30,250

Figure 7.2   2001 Urban agency service rep salary ranges

POSITION	SALARY RANGE
Personal CSR 2+ years	$25,848-$32,676
Personal CSR Under 2 years	$20,304-$22,039
Commercial CSR 7+ years	$33,877-$41,082
Commercial CSR 2 to 7 years	$28,956-$31,388
Commercial CSR Under 2 years	$22,642-$26,001
Employee Benefits CSR	$27,358-$32,449

Let's assume a company has a total sales cost of $3,000,000 and company-employed sales people are paid $75,000 plus a 4% commission on each sale. The average independent sales person is paid a 7% commission, plus an allowance for administrative costs of $25,000. Here, "x" represents the break-even level of sales:

$$0.04x + \$3,000,000 = 0.07x + \$25,000$$
$$\$2,975,000 = 0.03x$$
$$\$99,166,667 = x$$

Therefore, break-even sales are $99,166,167, below which the company should use the independent sales force and above which it should use a dedicated force, as illustrated in Figure 7.3.[3]

Figure 7.3   Factors determining choice of sales force

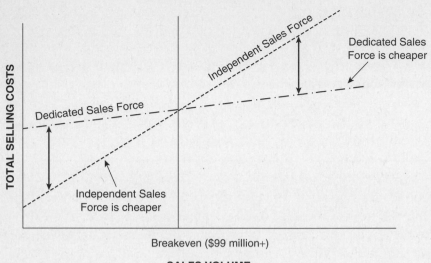

WHAT IT MEANS AND POTENTIAL CHALLENGES

When company management are considering hiring an independent sales representative or agency, cost is usually a critical consideration. As this analysis illustrates, independent sales representatives are cost-effective to a certain level. But cost is not the only consideration for sales management when weighing their options. In the 1990s, Nike's ACG (outdoor products) division used a combination of company-sales people (called "in-line") and an independent sales force because the in-line sales people knew Nike's strategic retail accounts best (such as Footlocker, FootAction, SportMart), while the contracted independent sales force were experts in the outdoor market and had relationships with leading retailers specializing in outdoor products (hiking shoes, trail shoes, cycling footwear, outdoor sandals). Nike needed the credibility with the outdoor retailers provided by the independent sales force's expertise in that market.

A company-employed sales force is expensive since the company is paying salary and fully loaded benefits (salary, bonus, medical and insurance benefits, and so on), even as sales cycles inevitably increase and decrease. But where a company-employed sales force is also going to be more loyal and devoted to the company's products, an independent sales force is representing products from multiple companies and may give greater prominence to those products that are easiest to sell. However, a proven independent sales force provides a significant boost to the company by generating sales at a lower cost. Furthermore, in line with how it would motivate its own sales force, company management can alter incentives to facilitate better cooperation and performance from the independent team.

Another key challenge for company management when evaluating the attractiveness of hiring independent sales representatives concerns control. Company-employed sales representatives are selected and trained in the company's practices, culture and style and, as alluded to above, develop loyalty to their firm and its products; independent representatives do not have the same level of allegiance. Their loyalty is to their compensation and how best and most quickly they can achieve desired income levels with minimal effort. A potential mismatch may occur, therefore, between a company's strategic goals and those of the independent sales representatives.

Control issues can also occur in the transition from an independent sales force to a company-owned one. Company management must determine how to maintain momentum when the transition occurs. This cannot be done at the time of the transition, so advance planning is a necessity to obviate the high risk of disruption with customers who have built relationships with the independent sales representatives.

There is no clear-cut resolution, nor should this analysis be used to arrive at one. Sales management need to consider the situation in which their company operates and factor in longer-term strategic goals. Costs will influence their decision, but other, harder-to-control factors, such as dedication and loyalty, may dictate the long-term success sought. A careful review of their company's core competencies is warranted as well to determine if the company's culture and decision-making processes would allow an independent sales agency to flourish, or flounder.

Endnotes

[1] Adapted from: Cron, W. L., T. E. DeCarlo and D. J. Palrymple. *Sales Management*, John Wiley & Sons, Inc., 2004: pp. 253–254

[2] http://www.insurancejournal.com/magazines/west/2001/03/26/features/21987.htm

[3] Adapted from Cron et al, op. cit.

Percentage of Sales

THE DEFINITION

Sales management are responsible for increasing revenues (total sales) by selling more products, developing new customers, or both. In this effort, reaching a target revenue goal results from getting existing sales representatives to sell more than they did last year, hiring new sales representatives to grow the business by selling more products and/or reaching new customers, or both. Sales management can determine the optimal size of the sales force based on a "percentage of sales" objective. The sales figure used in the calculation is derived from planned revenues in the forecast for the coming period (usually one year).

THE FORMULA AND ITS COMPONENTS[1]

The percentage-of-sales measurement is calculated using the following steps:

- Forecast planned revenues

- Determine percentage of sales based on industry standards, the firm's own historical performance, or a combination of both

- Develop a budget for management and field sales representatives.

WHERE'S THE DATA?

Forecast planned revenues will be based on senior management's goals for the coming year. This figure is determined from a combination of the previous year's results, internal growth goals, investors' expectations, industry growth projections and any new products or customer-segment objectives set out by senior management.

The percentage-of-sales figure is based on the company's own historical percentage, as well as any industry standards that exist, plus the company's own objectives for the coming year. For example, the company may decide that both its own historical percentage-of-sales figure and that of the industry are insufficient to achieve the coming year's growth objectives. Therefore, management will exercise judgment based on how far they believe they can push their own sales force to reach the goals. Any shortfall will need to be addressed by hiring additional reps and increasing the percentage-of-sales figure beyond historical industry or company standards. The sales force budget is likewise developed with consideration to these same factors.

CALCULATING IT

Let's assume that a New York-based food manufacturer of classic New York hot dogs had sales of $50 million last year and anticipates 20% growth next year, to $60 million in sales. It sells to retail chains and individual sidewalk vendors, and the industry average for the cost of the sales force as a percentage of total sales is 3.6%. The company's sales budget is divided into management (20%), field sales (75%) and support staff (5%). Based on this, we can now determine the size of the sales force by first calculating:

- Sales force budget
- Sales force percentage
- Sales force dollars.

Sales force budget

$$SFB = PR \times FSR$$

Where

SFB = sales force budget
PR = projected revenues
FSR = field sales ratio (based on industry average)
SFB = $60,000,000 \times 0.036$
      = $2,160,000

Sales force percentage

SFP = FS + SS

Where

SFP = sales force percentage
FS = field sales percentage of budget dollars
SS = support staff percentage of budget dollars
SFP = 0.75 + 0.05
    = 0.80

Sales force dollars

SFD = SFB × SFP

Where

SFD = sales force dollars
SFB = sales force budget
SFP = sales force percentage
SFD = $2,160,000 × 0.80
    = $1,728,000

If the average sales person in this company (or industry) costs $75,000 (including salary, bonus, commission and benefits — also known as "fully loaded" costs), then we can calculate the number of sales people the company can afford, as follows:

$$SFS = \frac{SFD}{SFC}$$

Where

SFS = sales force size
SFD = sales force dollars
SFC = sales force costs

$$SFS = \frac{\$1,728,000}{\$75,000}$$
$$= 23$$

If the company had 20 people last year, then three additional people would be required.

WHAT IT MEANS AND POTENTIAL CHALLENGES

Sales management may find this tool useful for planning purposes and to justify an expansion in their team. However, management should also consider whether the gain in sales can be accomplished by altering compensation incentives of the existing team, realigning territories or shifting responsibilities among the existing team members. Hiring new people adds a sizable potential cost to the sales budget and, if the forecast numbers are not met, then the sales organization's performance will be worse than before, since new people would have been added but without generating new sales. The pressure will then be on sales management either to quickly increase sales, thereby putting additional stress on the field sales force, or terminate some of their sales reps, potentially damaging morale within the company.

The use of industry standards is rarely a practical benchmark, attractive though it may be for planning purposes. Industry standards use averages; but often companies within an industry have significantly different operating standards, sizes and financial requirements, distorting the averages. Figure 8.1 provides data on the average sales force costs across industries.

If a company is noticeably different from its industry average, then management would be wise to analyze the possible reasons for the variation, keeping its own context firmly in mind. For example, if traditional PC manufacturers compare their percentage of sales to the industry average, they may be in for a shock since the industry average would include figures from low-cost operators like Dell. Yet trying to match Dell's figure would materially harm the company's competitive position since fewer sales people would be used to achieve the same level of sales. In this case, the challenge for Dell's competitors is not related to sales force cost, but instead lies in their operating model — a far more daunting and complex challenge to address.

Figure 8.1 Cross-industry comparison of sales-force costs

Company Size	Sales Force Total Cost as a Percentage of Sales	Industry	Sales Force Total Cost as a Percentage of Sales
Under $5 million	14.7%	Business Services	1.7%
$5-$25 million	10.5%	Chemicals	2.9%
$25-$100 million	7.9%	Communications	9.8%
$100-$250 million	3.5%	Educational Services	47.9%
Over $250 million	6.8%	Electronics	4.2%
		Fabricated Metals	10.8%
Product or Service		Health Services	19.9%
Industrial Products	4.1%	Hotels & Other Lodgings	21.4%
Industrial Services	6.4%	Instruments	2.3%
Office Products	9.4%	Machinery	10.1%
Office Services	8.1%	Manufacturing	13.6%
Consumer Products	5.4%	Office Equipment	9.0%
Consumer Services	7.9%	Paper & Allied Products	6.8%
		Printing & Publishing	12.0%
		Retail	6.1%
		Trucking & Warehousing	12.2%
		Wholesale (Consumer Goods)	3.7%
		Wholesale (Industrial Goods)	9.5%
		Average	6.9%

Source: Cron, W. L., T. E. De Carlo and D. J. Palrymple. *Sales Management*, John Wiley & Sons, Inc., 2004: p.115.

Endnote

[1] Adapted from Cron, W. L., T. E. DeCarlo and D. J. Palrymple. *Sales Management*, John Wiley & Sons, Inc., 2004: pp. 114–115.

Additional Reference

Davis, J. *Measuring Marketing: 103 Key Metrics Every Marketer Needs*, John Wiley & Sons (Asia) Pte Ltd., 2007.

MAG1C NUM8ER

9

Turnover Rate

THE DEFINITION

Turnover is the number of staff that depart during a specific period of time. The turnover rate expresses this figure in percentage terms.

THE FORMULA AND ITS COMPONENTS[1]

The turnover rate calculates the number of sales staff departures, voluntary or involuntary, relative to the total number of sales staff, multiplied by 100 (to convert it to a percentage):

$$TR = \frac{D_t \times 100}{F_t}$$

Where

TR = turnover rate
D_t = number of departures during time period t
F_t = total sales force size (the average during time period t)

WHERE'S THE DATA?

The turnover records are kept in the human resources department, whose managers compile personnel statistics for each department, including new hires and terminations. Each sales territory should also have its own employee records.

CALCULATING IT

If a company has 1,000 sales people worldwide and 75 depart over the course of one year, then the turnover rate is 7.5%:

$$TR = \frac{75 \times 100}{1,000}$$
$$= 7.5\%$$

WHAT IT MEANS AND POTENTIAL CHALLENGES

Departures of sales people can be expensive since management invests time, money and training into recruiting and retaining sales staff. When sales people leave, especially top performers, they take knowledge (about the company, its products and its strategy, as well as insight into their own territories about customers and market dynamics) to another firm. Therefore, reducing turnover is an important need for sales management.

However, turnover is inevitable as organizations change. The turnover rate should be reviewed in light of the company's strategic objectives to determine if the results are "acceptable". Industry and competitor comparisons may be part of the company's sales review, but there is a need for caution here because these statistics are based on averages and may offer little practical guidance given the unique circumstances of the individual company. A low turnover percentage may sound great from the HR and expense perspectives, but it may also signal that the company is overly generous with its compensation, loose with its performance standards or sales management has a hard time identifying and replacing under-performing people.

Turnover comprises several components:

- Death
- Involuntary departure (i.e. termination)
- Voluntary departure (i.e. recruitment by another company)
- Retirement
- Internal transfer.

Death, of course, is a form of involuntary departure and the least controllable factor, and should not be a key management concern. Termination results from poor performance, poor sales rep/company fit, illegal or unethical behavior, or job loss due to company-wide cutbacks. Sales management can minimize such turnover if their recruiting and candidate-selection criteria are clear, the interview process involves managers and colleagues from several departments, and a thorough background check is conducted. Voluntary departure may be within management's control if they are familiar with their sales people and can identify the source of dissatisfaction before it grows into a problem. Sales management may decide to respond by improving financial compensation, promoting, changing responsibilities or offering other, non-financial, benefits (more days of paid vacation, for example). Any of these decisions will be weighted against the potential future value expected from the sales reps most likely to depart. Retirements are less likely to be a significant challenge for savvy sales management since they will have anticipated these months or even years ahead, allowing time for recruiting new sales people and for succession planning. However, early retirement — perhaps for personal reasons — may spring the occasional surprise.

In each of these instances, sales management must decide whether replacement is warranted or if the departing person's responsibilities can be reassigned to other members of the sales team.

The impact of turnover can cost the company money in other ways. A 2004 report by "Better Jobs Better Care", a U.S.-based program funded by the Atlantic Philanthropies and The Robert Wood Johnson Foundation, outlined the following additional costs related to turnover:[2]

Direct costs, including:

- Cost of separation from the company

- Cost of vacancy

- Cost of replacement

- Cost of training and orientation

- Cost associated with an increased number of injured workers.

Indirect costs, including:

- Lost productivity until a replacement is trained

- Cost arising from reduced service quality

- Clients lost to other agencies as a result of a deterioration in image

- Cost arising from a deterioration in organizational culture and staff morale causing an adverse impact on the company's reputation and service quality and thus further increasing turnover.

Costs at service-delivery level, including:

- Consumer/Clients

  - Reduction in quality of care and quality of life

  - Care hours not provided

- Workers

  - Increased number of injuries to workers

  - Increased physical and emotional stress

  - Deterioration in working conditions leading to increased likelihood to quit.

Third-party payer costs, including:

- Under-funding of care services due to financial drain of turnover

- Illnesses and injuries attributable to reduced service quality

- Increased downstream medical costs arising from illnesses and injuries attributable to reduced service quality

- Higher levels of institutionalization of clients as a result of insufficient community-based staffing and quality of care.

Given the expense related to turnover, sales managers should conduct diligent and thorough evaluations of the causes of their organization's turnover to determine areas for improvement.

Endnotes

[1] http://www.tutor2u.net/business/people/workforce_turnover.asp
[2] Adapted from: http://www.bjbc.org/content/docs/TOCostReport.pdf

Additional References

For additional insight and formulas about turnover, visit: http://www.uwex.edu/ces/cced/publicat/turn.html#calc

Davis, J. *Measuring Marketing: 103 Key Metrics Every Marketer Needs*, John Wiley & Sons (Asia) Pte Ltd., 2007.

10

Recruiting

THE DEFINITION

Recruiting describes the effort sales management puts into identifying, attracting and hiring new sales personnel.

THE FORMULA AND ITS COMPONENTS[1]

The following formula can be used to determine the scope of the recruiting effort:

$$R = \frac{H}{S \times A}$$

Where

R = recruiting
H = new hires required
S = percentage of recruits selected
A = percentage who accept

WHERE'S THE DATA?

Recruiting data will come from the following sources:

• The hiring company's human resources (HR) department, which often keeps track of previous applicants, usually for a few months after a hiring period. When new sales positions need to be filled, then these previous applicants may serve as a good starting point for recruiting.

HR will have historical information on the company's past recruiting results, including information on the total number of people who applied, the number of people actually interviewed, the number offered jobs and the final number of those who accepted offers. Each of these can be converted into percentages that can help sales management determine the size and scope of the recruiting effort needed for the next hiring cycle.

- Company or industry job fairs, which attract those looking for sales positions. While not all job seekers are qualified, job fairs provide an additional source of prospective talent.

- Industry trade publications, which regularly research and write about the latest statistics in their industry, can provide sales management with useful information about competitors and market needs. Sales management can use this information to assess their own company's performance against the rest of the industry. Furthermore, they can use the information to determine if the numbers and quality of sales people they need are realistic, given the current state of the industry.

CALCULATING IT

An illustration will help:

- Company X needs 25 new sales people

- Past experience indicates 20% of those who apply will be offered positions

- HR statistics suggest that 75% of those offered a new position will accept

Simply plug in the data:

$$R = \frac{25}{(0.20) \times (0.75)}$$
$$= 167$$

Based on these statistics, a minimum of 167 people would need to apply if the company wants to fill the 25 positions.

What It Means and Potential Challenges

With sales people filling a vital role (growing revenues, profits and customers), identifying and recruiting the best talent is one of sales management's most important tasks. Sales management may lead their own recruiting effort or, more likely, will work with the HR department to coordinate the recruiting efforts. Since recruiting the right talent is rarely a 1:1 ratio (one applicant leads to one hire), determining the number of applicants required to be able to fill the vacant positions is needed.

Recruiting is an important activity and sales management must carefully plan the time and resources required to do an effective job. In this basic example, 167 applicants may be a large number to review if the organization is small or medium-sized. On the other hand, if you are IBM, then the number of people available from human resources and field sales is large enough that the responsibilities can be distributed with lower disruption to regular work activities. No matter how large the organization, recruiting requires a keen sense of the following:

- The company's culture

- The personalities that would fit the company's culture

- The skills being sought

- A clear process that is explained upfront for the recruit

- A thoughtful description of the job

- A set of interview questions designed to identify the best possible candidates

- The professional will to stick to the company's overall recruiting standards and not settle on anyone less qualified than required.

Sales management should be aware of the applicant's career aspirations and be able to confidently describe growth opportunities if the new recruit succeeds on the job. Sales people thrive on challenges, rewards, recognition and future opportunities, so sales management should ensure that these areas are discussed. The risk in not anticipating the ambitions of successful sales people is that they may leave to join a competitor, and the time and money invested in attracting, hiring and training them will be lost. Sales people who leave the company to join a competitor will also take with them knowledge of the company's strategic plans for the next couple of years, creating a potential competitive disadvantage.

Endnote

[1] Adapted from: Cron, W. L., T. E. DeCarlo and D. J. Palrymple. *Sales Management*, John Wiley & Sons, Inc., 2004: p. 324.

Additional Reference

Davis, J. *Measuring Marketing: 103 Key Metrics Every Marketer Needs,* John Wiley & Sons (Asia) Pte Ltd., 2007.

Breakdown Approach

THE DEFINITION

The breakdown approach is a method for determining size of sales force using current economic forecasts, estimates of market potential (economic and/or demographic), and company expectations of growth extrapolated from baseline sales.

THE FORMULA AND ITS COMPONENTS

To determine sales force size using the breakdown approach, sales professionals must know their previous sales history, projections of their own new sales for the coming year, and market forecasts.[1] Sales force size is calculated using the following formula.[2]

$$SFS = \frac{FS}{SPP}$$

Where

SFS = sales force size
FS = forecast sales
SPP = average sales per person

WHERE'S THE DATA?

Forecast sales figures are found in the business plan for each time period, usually one year. Sales forecasts are based on the previous year's sales plus an adjustment for inflation, market changes (usually industry and customer growth or, in rare instances, retraction) and internal estimates of the company's growth from a combination of previous history and the expected growth rate, which may be different from recent history as a result of new product launches or new segment opportunities. Data on average sales per person is found in sales reports that summarize recent performance. The aggregate dollar figure is divided by the number of sales people during the given period to arrive at a per-person total.

CALCULATING IT

To determine sales force size, sales management must first develop total forecast sales for the year. To illustrate,[3] let's assume that a beverage company had sales of $100 million last year and management wants to know the size of the sales force needed to succeed in the current year. Because of the nature of the company's contracts with its distributors, all existing business will be renewed for the coming year. Furthermore, the company has confirmed a new distributor contract for $5 million. Research indicates the overall market will grow 15% this year. To summarize:

Sales, previous year	= $100,000,000
New distributor contracts, current year	= $5,000,000
Preliminary sales forecast, current year	= $105,000,000
Projected total market growth	= 15%

The company's current year's sales forecast is the sum of last year's sales plus this year's expected new contracts plus projected market growth:

$$FS = CYF + MG \text{ (in dollars)}$$

Where

FS = current year's forecast sales
CYF = current year preliminary sales forecast
MG = market growth in dollars

Therefore,

$$FS = \$105,000,000 + \$15,750,000$$
$$= \$120,750,000$$

At this stage, the company can now determine if its existing sales force is the right size or if it needs to increase or decrease it based on the total forecast sales. Last year, the company had 100 sales people. The average sales person generated sales of $1 million ($100,000,000 ÷ 100). To maintain $1 million of sales per person, this company must have 121 sales people, a 21% increase in the size of its sales force:

Average sales per person $= \$1,000,000$

$$\text{Sales force size} = \frac{\$120,750,000}{\$1,000,000}$$

$$= 121$$

WHAT IT MEANS AND POTENTIAL CHALLENGES

As a company's business grows, servicing existing and new customers successfully is both a responsibility and an ongoing challenge for the field sales force. Every company is different, and bases its sales planning on corporate sales objectives (volume or profit-oriented, customer loyalty or new-customer acquisition) and market conditions (customer needs, competitor tactics, economic and demographic trends). Sales managers design their tactical go-to-market plans around maximizing the potential financial returns from their targeted customer base, so determining how many sales people are needed to service existing customers and attract new customers is a critical decision that can directly influence whether a company achieves its sales targets.

The breakdown approach is useful for determining the size of the sales force required, but sales professionals must be careful not to depend solely on the previous year's average sales per person as a benchmark for future sales needs. As business grows, companies seek to improve both efficiency and effectiveness, which includes establishing growth targets for existing sales people. The example in this chapter simplifies a common sales management challenge: how to inspire the sales force to achieve these new growth targets yet not demotivate them by being overly aggressive. The breakdown approach might lure sales management into the comfortable world of maintaining existing sales standards ($1 million of sales per person in this case). While the field sales force may find the new goals a relief, since they only have to maintain the same level of sales as last year (it is the number of new representatives hired that drives growth in this case), it offers little long-term challenge, and the risk of complacency grows over time. Conversely, if the same 100 sales people are asked to achieve the new $120.75 million target, then the 21% sales increase required may be too formidable, leading to reduced motivation.

Sales management must look at the factors contributing to the projected sales increase. Sales data for the previous year's sales are found in the annual report. Expected market growth can be obtained from economic forecasts for the company's specific industry. And projected customer growth can be learned from market-research data, including customer survey information. Each of these will affect the sales management's decision on the right balance between sales-force size requirements and projected sales growth.

Endnotes

[1] http://www.busmgt.ulst.ac.uk/h_mifflin/glossary/glossary.html
[2] http://futrell-www.tamu.edu/SM_OUTLINE_CHAPTER6.doc
[3] http://www.va-interactive.com/inbusiness/editorial/sales/ibt/ales_fo.html

Additional References

Bangs, Jr., D. H. *The Market Planning Guide*, Upstart Publishing Co., 1998.
Bangs, Jr., D. H. *The Start Up Guide,* Upstart Publishing Co., 1989.
Burstiner, I. *The Small Business Handbook,* Simon & Schuster Inc., 1997.
Davis, J. *Measuring Marketing: 103 Key Metrics Every Marketer Needs,* John Wiley & Sons (Asia) Pte Ltd., 2007.
Evetts, J. *Seven Pillars of Sales Success,* Sterling Publishing Co., 1990.
Leza, R. L. and Placencia, J. *Develop Your Business Plan,* The Oasis Press, 1988.
Resnik, P. *The Small Business Bible,* John Wiley & Sons, Inc., 1988.
http://www.allbusiness.com/periodicals/article/123857-1.html
http://futrell-www.tamu.edu/fos%20chapter%2016.doc
http://highered.mcgraw-hill.com/sites/0072398868/student_view0/chapter16/chapter_outline.html

12 Workload Approach

THE DEFINITION

The workload approach is a method for determining sales force size based on the size of customer accounts and the concomitant amount of work required to service the customer successfully. Customers are segmented into account classes, based on account size, allowing sales management to determine and then deploy the right number of sales personnel required to ensure that the customer's needs are met.

THE FORMULA AND ITS COMPONENTS

The workload approach organizes customers into common groups, usually based on account size. Management then determines how many sales people are required to call on the various customer groups.[1] There are three workload approaches that will be discussed here.

Approach 1[2]

The workload approach calculates sales force size as follows:

$$SFS = \frac{SE}{SEapp}$$

Where

SFS = sales force size
SE = total selling effort needed (total calls to be made)

SEapp = average selling effort per sales person (average total calls made per sales person)

WHERE'S THE DATA?

The total calls to be made are projections from each year's planning and budgeting cycle for the upcoming year. Sales management either develops their own sales revenue target or are given one by senior management. The revenue target is translated into targets for each region, territory/office and individual sales representative, including estimates for the number of calls needed to ultimately achieve the target. There is no precise science to estimating the number of calls, but seasoned sales professionals generally have a strong sense of the total calls/converted sales ratio from past experience. This figure can also be determined by reviewing the sales patterns from competitors in the industry, although these figures are usually not publicly reported unless a trade publication has conducted general industry research. The total sales calls per person is simply another ratio: total sales calls (during a given time period)/total number of sales people during the same time period.

CALCULATING IT

Networked marketing companies (such as Amway and Mary Kay) offer a useful illustration of this workload approach. Networked marketing companies generate sales through large networks of independent sales representatives. Each sales representative generates income from a combination of product sales and the sales from other representatives they have recruited into the organization. (This recruited organization is also known as the "downstream sales team".) Let's assume that a hypothetical sales representative — Barbara — has identified 3,000 new customers in her territory that she wants to reach in the next 30 days to achieve her sales objectives. She must now determine the number of sales people required.

First, Barbara would outline the facts as she knows them:

Total number of customers = 3,000
Duration (in days)   = 30

Next, she needs to determine the denominator (average selling effort per prospective sales person) by dividing the number of customers to be reached by the number of days required:

Total selling effort needed

$$\text{Number of calls required} = \frac{3,000}{30}$$
$$= 100$$

Finally, Barbara can now determine the number of sales people she needs by dividing the total selling effort needed by the average calls made per sales person:

$$\text{SFS} = \frac{\text{SE}}{\text{SEapp}}$$

$$= \frac{3,000}{100}$$

$$\doteq 30 \text{ sales people}$$

From a practical point of view, it is likely that not all of Barbara's new hires will stay the entire 30 days (perhaps due to the type of work, challenges with customers or finding another job). She should factor in a turnover rate to ensure she can get the equivalent of 30 sales people's work for 30 days. Each industry turnover rate differs, but Barbara determines that 20% is normal for network marketing. Therefore, her calculation is refined:

$$\text{Turnover rate} = 30 \times 0.20$$
$$= 6 \text{ (added to the original forecast of 30 people)}$$
$$= 36 \text{ sales people required}$$

Approach 2[3]

A slight variation on the first approach is outlined in the sequential steps below:

A. Identify the total number of calls needed or customers to be reached (3,000, in Barbara's case)

B. Determine time needed per call (roughly 1.6 hours per call in this case, derived from 100 calls per sales person divided by 20 days in a working month, assuming an eight-hour day)

C. Determine total working time (A. × B.) (4,800 hours in this case)

D. Determine actual selling time available per sales person (160 hours — based on eight hours per day x 20 days)

E. Determine number of sales people (C. ÷ D.) (4,800 ÷ 160 = 30)

Once again, Barbara would want to consider a turnover rate.

Approach 3[4]

An alternative workload method is known as "reach-frequency", and it is represented by the following:

$$FTE = \frac{reach \times frequency}{capacity}$$

Where

FTE   = full-time employees
reach   = number of customers to be reached
frequency = customer visits during the sales period

Let's assume that Barbara and her team have identified 10,000 potential customers in four different segments:

Figure 12.1   Breakdown of segments

Customers	Reach	Frequency	Calls
Segment 1	3,000	2	6,000
Segment 2	2,500	2	5,000
Segment 3	2,500	1	2,500
Segment 4	2,000	1	2,000
Total	10,000		15,500

The average sales representative has a total sales capacity of 100 calls (20 selling days $\times$ 5 calls per day).

Using the formula, we can then determine the size of the sales force required:

$$FTE = \frac{15,500}{100}$$

$$= 155 \text{ sales reps.}$$

Clearly, Barbara's sales force needs have changed, but so too have the assumptions. The first two approaches assumed one call per potential customer, but not all customers will buy on the first contact. In fact, most will not. The reach-frequency method provides more guidance when the assumed number of customer visits before a sale is made is larger than one. Of course, the numbers from the previous two approaches can certainly be used to illustrate Approach 3:

Figure 12.2 Calculating sales-force size using Approach 3

Customers	Reach	Frequency	Calls
Segment 1 Total	3,000	1	3,000

$$FTE = \frac{3,000}{100}$$

$$= 30 \text{ sales reps needed}$$

WHAT IT MEANS AND POTENTIAL CHALLENGES

Sales plans usually include a projection of the total work required to achieve a goal. The challenge lies in the cost of reaching the goal: sales people are expensive. The leaders of any business want to keep costs low to maximize profits while maintaining good relations with customers. It can be a vexing challenge. The need, therefore, is to determine the right size for the sales force given the amount of work to be done.

The workload approach is useful, particularly with less-complex, higher-volume products such as consumer goods, since established practices and expectations exist between product manufacturers, sales reps and customers (whether consumers, in the case of network marketing businesses; or channel accounts, in the case of traditional consumer-products distribution). The reason is that metrics exist from years of industry practice, and management can approximate the number of customers they need to reach to achieve a certain level of sales. The workload approach becomes more challenging with more complex products (industrial machinery and software technologies, for example) since achieving the sales objective depends on qualitative factors such as the depth of the relationship with the customers and the amount of customization required to complete a sale. These variables are hard to pin down numerically but are, nevertheless, important in this type of sale. Also, the workload approach focuses only on the costs (or investment) made, and not the return. More complex management issues such as pricing, marketing communications and promotion programs, market-share goals and training expenses are ignored. Sales management must also consider these factors when determining sales force sizing.

Finally, knowing the amount of work and the number of sales people required to complete the work are part of the overall sales-force development objectives, but should not be the only criteria for determining the final composition of the sales force. The workload approach does not account for the type of sales skills or personality needed, which are important factors as management considers how best to develop the sales force to achieve company goals.

Endnotes

[1] Adapted from http://grader.prenhall.com/BB_CGI/BB_Grader/1,1002,,.html
[2] Adapted from http://www.business.txstate.edu/users/ds60/296,36,Sales Force Size: Analytical Tools
[3] http://classwork.busadm.mu.edu/Andrews/MARK%20140/PPTch16.ppt
[4] http://www.bayser.com/SalesForceStrategy.htm

Additional References

Davis, J. *Measuring Marketing: 103 Key Metrics Every Marketer Needs,* John Wiley &
    Sons (Asia) Pte Ltd., 2007.
http://nsslha.org/about/continuing-ed/ASHA-courses/SSA/SSA6710.htm
www.embarcadero.com/resources/tech_papers/managing_sql_server_performance_
    with_performance_analyst.pdf
http://www-rohan.sdsu.edu/~renglish/377/notes/chapt16/

13 Price

THE DEFINITION

Price is the monetary value of a good, service or asset. Price has a significant influence on a company's success since revenues result from a specific number of units sold multiplied by a price charged. Price influences customers' perceptions as well. Low price usually conveys a perception of a cheaper, lower-quality product, whereas higher prices connote better quality and, at the highest prices, premium and/or exclusive products.

THE FORMULA AND ITS COMPONENTS

To ensure a common effort, marketing and sales management should agree on their approach *before* going to market. The matrix[1] below outlines four general price strategies (not exhaustive):

Figure 13.1   The price-strategy matrix

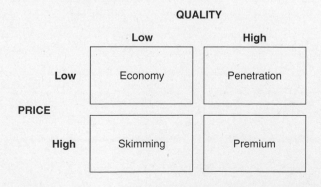

Economy pricing entails charging a small mark-up above cost.

Penetration pricing describes the price companies charge when trying to gain market share. Companies charge the lowest possible price to gain share while still making a profit or, at a minimum, breaking even. Cost or production efficiencies allow this kind of pricing to work, but the challenge is in sustaining the cost efficiencies and advantages over time.

In the 1980s, Japanese and Korean microchip makers[2] were selling their products below cost to gain share in a pricing practice known as "dumping". This led to anti-dumping complaints from the U.S. Department of Commerce against the Japanese and Korean firms as well as an anti-dumping lawsuit filed by the U.S. Government. Dumping and penetration pricing are not the same.

Skimming is when the highest possible price that the market will bear relative to competitors' offerings is charged for a product or service. It is often used in the early stages of market development for a new product, when the quality of offerings in the overall market is low as a result of the market's immaturity. As the market matures, if the company maintains a quality edge as competitors enter, then its pricing strategy would shift to premium.

Premium pricing describes the highest possible price charged over time, and arises from the company's dominant market-share position, unusually high-quality products and corresponding image, and a unique offering in the market.

Once marketers have planned their pricing strategy, they can then run a simple calculation to determine if a retail price yields a satisfactory net price once discounts and taxes are included:

$$P = P_L - D - A - T$$

Where

P = price (the final price realized)

P_L = list price (the target full retail price)

D = discounts (percentage reduction from list price, usually based on volume)

A = allowances (price reductions issued for trade-ins and/or promotional dollars from cooperative marketing activities between the manufacturer and retailer)

T = taxes and tariffs

WHERE'S THE DATA?

List price is determined based on the company's historical prices for comparable products, competitors' pricing for similar products, cost recovery for developing the product, positioning requirements (is it a low-end mass-market product or a high-end luxury good?) and feedback from customers on what they are willing to pay. This feedback is provided by market research, including surveys and focus groups. Discounts are set by company management, usually before a product is first introduced to the market, then adapted over time as business conditions and customer response warrant. Companies establish percentage discounts at different quantities, allowing buyers the flexibility of purchasing more of the product at a cheaper per-unit price. Allowance data is derived from historical practices and relationships with key customer accounts. Company management will tailor allowance and discount programs for each customer since buying patterns and needs differ among customers. Tax and benefits data are found in government and regulatory code books and websites, and from tax and accounting experts.

CALCULATING IT

Let's assume the sales person's product has a suggested retail price of $10. Taxes and tariffs imposed by the tax authorities amount to 5%. The sales person decides a promotion program is needed to induce more sales, with the following offer:

• Discounts that average 5%

• Allowances that average 2%.

The calculation is thus:

$$P = \$10 - \$0.50 - \$0.20 - \$0.50 = \$8.80$$

Therefore, the list price of $10 nets out to $8.80 per product sold.

The sales person may want marketing to test this pricing level with a selection of the company's best customers. An online-survey approach is chosen to maximize the potential responses (since it is relatively inexpensive to develop an online survey that is accessible on the Internet, where it can be seen by potentially millions of people). Let's assume three price variations are included in the test:

Figure 13.2   Price/orders/revenue comparisons

Price (before discounts and taxes)	$5	$10	$20
Orders	1,000	1,500	900
Revenue	$5,000	$15,000	$18,000

In this case, the middle price of $10 produces the highest number of orders while the $20 price produces the highest revenues. Sales management, in conjunction with marketing and senior management's business expectations, must decide which is more important: the number of customers or the revenue generated from a smaller group of premium buyers. The answer will depend on the marketing strategy and overall business objectives, as well as the company's (or product's) image and position in the market. Furthermore, each region of a given country may have different price needs since the economic conditions in each region vary.

WHAT IT MEANS AND POTENTIAL CHALLENGES

All of the price components described could have been altered to encourage demand: lower list price; higher discounts to inspire the retailer to buy larger quantities; higher allowances to encourage more promotion and support from the retailer, and so on. Marketers and sales management have no control over taxes and tariffs, but they do need to factor them into their final pricing analysis and recommendations. If the marketer's goal was to maximize profit and position the product as a premium product, then the $20 suggested price is the most appropriate and sales management should strive to meet that target.

A pricing strategy will include a consideration of the company's volume objectives, profit objectives or some other set of considerations such as competitive parity. If volume is the primary goal, then the marketing and sales efforts will pursue unit and/or market-share growth. Penetration pricing is the best approach in this case. This means setting price low enough to capture market share rapidly. This is most often used when competitors have identical, similar or better products. If the objective is profitability, then a skimming pricing strategy is most often used in the early market-development stages, adjusting over time to a premium pricing approach. This means that a company believes its product offering is unique and innovative and, consequently, has a probable lead over the competition. Companies price at a premium level both to capture higher profits and to establish and reinforce a market-leading position. Over time, sales management may encourage marketers to reduce the price as competition enters (which it will inevitably do, since competitors will notice a company's success and want to get their share of it as well), but this may risk dilution of the company's premium reputation. Alternatively, the marketer can opt for value-added changes in the product that keep its price at a premium level. Sales management would need to be convinced of the relevance of these changes to their customers before agreeing to this approach.

These are not the only pricing approaches. It is quite possible that a blended approach may be the most sensible, whereby a firm chooses to price mid-market. Once again, this decision must be considered in the context of a firm's overall positioning objectives. Often, a middle approach can become no-man's land in which the products are not perceived as either premium or mass market. Consequently, the consumer does not know what the product stands for. If a reasonable argument for this middle approach cannot be made, then consumers are likely to buy on the basis of either lowest cost or most unique features.

Pricing data should come from the company's business and sales plans for each product. Often, sales representatives control final price (usually within pre-set guidelines) because they are dealing directly with the customer at the point of sale and know first-hand what the customer is seeking. As each order comes in from the market, this information is fed directly into the company's financial reports, where the details of each transaction are fully described. Sales people should be recording the final agreed price and quantity figures accurately so that the accountants know how to categorize the price specifics. Depending on each company's accounting practices, allowances and discounts may be counted against marketing's programs budget, or they may be counted against the sales team directly, especially if each sales person's compensation is tied to measures of financial performance such as profitability. They could also be a combination of these methods.

Endnotes

[1] Doyle, C. *Collins Internet-Linked Dictionary of Marketing,* Harper Collins, 2003, 2006: p. 177.
[2] Adapted from: Shell, G. R., "Make the Rules or Your Rivals Will", 2004, Crown Business, Knowledge@Wharton Newsletter *How Companies Use (and Abuse) Law for Competitive Gains* http://knowledge.wharton.upenn.edu/article/978.cfm.

Additional References

Davis, J. *Magic Numbers for Consumer Marketing*, John Wiley & Sons (Asia) Pte Ltd., 2005: pp. 203–206.
Davis, J. *Measuring Marketing: 103 Key Metrics Every Marketer Needs*, John Wiley & Sons (Asia) Pte Ltd., 2007.
Dolan, R. J. "How Do You Know When the Price is Right?", *Harvard Business Review*, Sept-Oct (1995).
Usborne, N. "How to Determine the Best Price for Your Product or Service", February 14, 2006. http://www.marketingprofs.com/6/usborne6.asp.

14

Mark–Up Price[1]

THE DEFINITION

Proper pricing helps companies recover costs, position products and generate profits. When costs are known and the business plan stipulates specific margin targets for products, then mark-up pricing can be used to set price.

THE FORMULA AND ITS COMPONENTS

This pricing method adds a slight increase, or "mark-up", to the cost of the product or service. It is often used in professional-services businesses. Companies using it would calculate their base costs for a project or product, then add a percentage mark-up to reflect the premium they believe their product or service represents. This is represented by the following formula:

$$MUP = \frac{UC}{(1 - ROSe)}$$

Where

MUP = mark-up price
UC   = unit cost
ROSe = expected return on sales (see Magic Number 50)

Unit cost must be determined to calculate the mark-up pricing formula. To calculate unit cost, use this formula:

$$UC = VC + \frac{FC}{US}$$

Where

UC = unit cost
VC = variable cost
FC = fixed cost
US = unit sales (in units, not dollars)

Professional-services firms often use mark-up pricing by estimating the total project cost, then adding in their profit, or mark-up.

Manufacturing operations have a similar approach that requires understanding certain key costs and sales estimates to calculate a cost per unit, from which the mark-up price can ultimately be determined.

WHERE'S THE DATA?

Variable costs change as quantities of product bought, sold and produced change. They comprise materials and other supplies that go into making a final product, and are found in suppliers' price lists, industry publications, and market-research studies. Fixed costs (rent, insurance, salaries, design, depreciation, utility fees, for example) do not change as quantities produced change. Fixed-cost data is found in company accounting summaries, where all costs are captured. Aggregate fixed costs are summarized in the income statement. Finance and/or accounting will have information on specific fixed costs allocated to the marketing and sales departments. As with all numbers that describe or affect marketing decisions, it is important to double-check accounting's figures against the assigned own budget figures to see what differences there are, if any. Usually, the accountants have specific rules that govern how to count certain costs and these tend to be more detailed than the basic budgets marketing departments (or most other departments, for that matter) would submit. It is quite likely that sales management's figures will not match the figures from accounting or finance, but that is probably as a consequence of these rules.

CALCULATING IT

In the following case, Company X makes upscale beverage bottles. The following are its expected costs and sales:

- Variable costs $5

- Fixed costs $100,000

- Expected unit sales   20,000

Company X positions its bottles at the premium end of the market because it uses premium materials, so while its costs are slightly higher than those of its competitors, it is able to command high prices because of the added value its products offer. Therefore, Company X expects a mark-up of 15%. Its pricing can now be calculated. First, we determine unit cost:

$$\text{Unit cost} = \text{variable costs} + \frac{\text{fixed costs}}{\text{unit sales}}$$

$$\text{Unit cost} = \$5 + \frac{\$100,000}{20,000}$$

$$= \$10$$

Next, we add this figure into the mark-up price equation:

$$\text{Mark-up price} = \frac{\text{unit cost}}{(1 - \text{expected return on sales})}$$

$$= \frac{\$20}{(1 - 0.2)}$$

$$= \$25$$

Company X's mark-up price to its retail accounts is $25. Its profit is $5 on each bottle sold.

WHAT IT MEANS AND POTENTIAL CHALLENGES

While mark-up pricing is generally simple, it is not the most effective approach to pricing. It is simple because you only need to estimate the mark-up you wish to earn above cost, and price accordingly. It is not always effective because you may not be maximizing your profit or sales potential. Perhaps the customer sees Company X's bottles as being of only mediocre value, despite the premium materials. If so, Company X is unlikely to hit its sales target. On the other hand, customers may perceive them as being of extraordinary value, even if priced at $50. Company X's marketers then have to consider whether they would sell just as many if the price were $5 or $10 higher, thereby improving their margins.

While mark-up pricing is simple, since it is really based on covering costs with the addition of a little margin, it may leave out any unique positioning opportunities that could help marketers build a more reputable, exclusive brand. Even if it was not marketing's goal to be a high-end brand, money may still be left on the table if mark-up pricing is the primary pricing guide.

Mark-up pricing is based on estimates of the total costs for a project or product and, therefore, the data can be found in the company's marketing plans and accounting budgets for each department. Identifying the costs is the tricky part, so a company's systems must be sophisticated enough to measure cost inputs, both fixed and variable, to the unit level. Once the costs are known, or estimated, then the marketing manager's job is to identify a reasonable mark-up price. This will most likely be driven by the company's strategic margin goals for each product line, as well as the positioning goals for each product in each product line. The reason for noting the positioning goals is that pricing has a direct impact on consumers' perceptions of a product's position vis-à-vis the competition.

Endnote

[1] Adapted from: Kotler, P., Siew, M. L., Swee H. A. and Tan C. T. *Marketing Management: An Asian Perspective,* Prentice Hall, 2003.

Additional References

Davis, J. *Magic Numbers for Consumer Marketing,* John Wiley & Sons (Asia) Pte Ltd., 2005: pp. 216–219.

Davis, J. *Measuring Marketing: 103 Key Metrics Every Marketer Needs,* John Wiley & Sons (Asia) Pte Ltd., 2007.

http://users.wbs.warwick.ac.uk/dibb_simkin/student/glossary/ch19.html

Target–Return Price[1]

THE DEFINITION

When the company's investment decisions are dictated by specific expectations on return, then price is set based on recovery of all costs plus a target return of investment.

THE FORMULA AND ITS COMPONENTS

Target-return price is designed to cover all costs and yield a specified or target return. Like mark-up pricing (Magic Number 14), it is another cost-based approach.

$$TRP = C_{pu} + \frac{R \times I}{US}$$

Where

TRP = target-return price

C_{pu} = cost per unit

R = expected return

I = capital invested

US = unit sales (in units)

WHERE'S THE DATA?

Data for cost per unit will either come from suppliers' price summaries or from internal production and operations plans. Expected return data is determined by the company's historical expectations on return as well as current investors' expectations, which can be significantly influenced by return-on-investment (ROI) conditions elsewhere in the market (whether higher or lower than ROI performance for the company in recent years). Capital invested is determined by growth plans, capital needs to fund the growth, current cash and cash equivalents, the state of capital markets and the attractiveness of the company's business proposition that is prompting the need for additional capital.

Additional data is found in the company finance and accounting departments. One of the formula's variables, capital invested, is located in the balance sheet under liabilities, either as shareholders' equity or long-term debt.

Unit sales are found, in their final form, in the income statement. However, since those are typically completed at the end of business cycles (quarterly or annually), preliminary figures can be found in sales or in the preliminary finance reports.

CALCULATING IT

Let's assume that an athletic-apparel company, Corner Kick, competing only in soccer apparel, decides to launch a new product to compete against Adidas and Nike. Sales are expected to be 100,000 units in the first year, but the company believes a new fabric machine is necessary to create the quality of product needed. Corner Kick's marketing manager wants to know what his target-return price would be by investing $3 million in the new fabric machine that would be used to blend two or more specialty fabrics together. Corner Kick's apparel has always been positioned as premium products sold at premium prices. The cost per unit is $35. Senior management has premium expectations on the target returns for the $3 million investment, seeking an ROI of 25%, which means the final price should return $750,000.

Here's how the analysis looks:

$$\text{Target-return price} = 35 + \frac{0.25 \times \$3,000,000}{100,000}$$

$$= \$42.50$$

Therefore, to achieve a 25% ROI, the target-return price must be at least $42.50.

What It Means and Potential Challenges

Target-return pricing depends on the assumptions and expectations that went into it. For example, if the expected ROI is not in line with industry standards on similar projects, then it is quite possible that the target-return price will not be adequate to meet the company's needs. It is also conceivable that the unit sales assumptions are off, perhaps significantly. In this event, it would be necessary to determine break-even at different sales volumes to see where a more accurate target-return price should be set. Keep in mind as well that target-return pricing ignores competitor pricing, customer response and market trends, all of which can affect the final analysis. Preparing multiple scenarios is often the key to selecting an approach with which you are most comfortable.

Endnote

[1] Adapted from: Kotler, P., M. L. Siew, H. A. Swee and C. T. Tan. *Marketing Management: An Asian Perspective*, Prentice Hall, 2003, p. 496.

Additional References

Davis, J. *Magic Numbers for Consumer Marketing*, John Wiley & Sons (Asia) Pte Ltd., 2005: pp. 220–221.

Davis, J. *Measuring Marketing: 103 Key Metrics Every Marketer Needs*, John Wiley & Sons (Asia) Pte Ltd., 2006.

http://www.marketingpower.com/mg-dictionary-view3143.php

Net Sales Contribution

THE DEFINITION

Net sales contribution calculates the financial sales contribution of a specific segment or sales territory to total sales for all segments or territories, expressed as a percentage. Note that territories can be defined geographically and/or in terms of customer or product type.

THE FORMULA AND ITS COMPONENTS

The formula for net sales contribution is:

$$S_{ni} = \frac{S_i}{S_t} \times 100$$

Where

S_{ni} = net sales contribution for segment or territory i
S_i = sales from segment or territory i
S_t = total sales from all segments or territories

WHERE'S THE DATA?

Sales data on each segment or territory is maintained by sales management. Most finance departments may also keep this level of detailed data, depending on the reporting criteria and requirements they use.

Figure 16.1   Segmented financial results[1] of Agrium Inc.

By Geography (US$ millions)					
		WHOLESALE			
	Retail	North America	South America	Other	Total
Net Sales	$1,114	$1,703	$143	($122)	$2,838
Net Sales Cont. %	39%	60%	5%	-4%	100%

By Product (US$ millions)						
	Ammonia	Urea	Nitrate, Sulfate	Phosphate	Potash	Total
Net Sales	$397	$499	$284	$309	$214	$1,703
Net Sales Cont. %	23%	29%	17%	18%	13%	100%

CALCULATING IT

To illustrate, a company has total sales of $100 million, with sales from territory A of $25 million. The net sales contribution of territory A is, therefore, 25%, as follows:

$$S_{ni} = \frac{\$25,000,000}{\$100,000,000} \times 100\%$$
$$= 25\%$$

Net sales contribution measures each segment's or territory's contribution to total sales, and can serve as an indicator for planning future sales and marketing strategies. To illustrate further, the 2004 annual report for Agrium Inc., a Canadian-based company specializing in the manufacture of agricultural nutrients and industrial products, gives detailed analysis of the respective contributions to net sales of each of its various activities, as shown below. This also gives shareholders a good idea of where the company's focus lies and where it is concentrating its efforts.

What It Means and Potential Challenges

Segmentation is an important tool to help marketers identify groups of customers with similar characteristics, for which they then develop specific marketing programs that appeal to each segment while also maintaining consistency with their company's goals. Segments are broadly organized around four common themes, and marketers want to understand more clearly how much each segment contributes to overall sales. The need, therefore, is to measure the specific sales contribution of each segmentation category:

- Demographics (age, ethnicity, sex, income…)

- Psychographics (behaviors, likes, needs, wants…)

- Geography (location)

- Product use (how the product or service is actually used by the customer).

Measuring net sales contribution helps marketers understand each segment's portion of total sales. It is a more general, less-detailed, indicator of performance, and serves as a useful starting point for further analysis when marketers wish to clarify the underlying factors of each segment's contribution, particularly as measured against the marketing plan for the time period under review. Using Agrium's figures above, a North American marketer would want to review his or her region's performance against the company's plan. Assuming the region performed better than expected, the marketer might then review the sales contributions of each product against the original plan to determine any variances. If, hypothetically, the urea product sales were significantly higher than the plan, then the marketer would want to research the underlying causes. A market-by-market, or even account-by-account (within North America), review of each product's sales would probably reveal where urea is gaining sales beyond expectations. The marketer might then modify the marketing plan to take advantage of this growing market opportunity, perhaps by developing new pricing programs, focusing sales resources toward winning more accounts of a particular type within the best growing regions, or encouraging the development of new products or product extensions based around the urea product category.

Knowing the performance of each segment helps marketers and their companies be more effective in their future marketing and product efforts, and net sales contribution is a valuable metric in this process.

Endnote

[1]http://calgwebe.agrium.com/ir2004AnnualReport/index.html

Additional Reference

Davis, J. *Measuring Marketing: 103 Key Metrics Every Marketer Needs*, John Wiley & Sons (Asia) Pte Ltd., 2007.

Part Two

SALES MANAGEMENT AND SELLING

Selling is both art and science, and both are required to achieve consistent success. The art of sales is concerned with the behavior and qualitative approaches each sales professional must adopt to be successful with clients. The science deals with determining a compensation system that inspires the right selling behavior and leads to the desired results. The effectiveness of the selling effort is reflected in the growth of business from customers, both current and new. Sales professionals will find numerous useful tools to help them assess their success with customers. In Part Two, we look at a range of metrics related to the remuneration of the sales force and which thus have a direct bearing on their individual and collective performance.

Good business is based on relationships that are beneficial to both the company and its customers. Here, we also highlight measures that companies should consider in their approach to customers and which will help them to establish and conduct business relationships that are both efficient and cost-effective.

Straight Commission

THE DEFINITION

A commission is a percentage of either the final sales price of a specific product or of the total dollar sales achieved by an individual sales person. Commission percentages will vary by industry and company. Furthermore, commissions are not fixed and can vary based on the goals set by management. Commission sales depend on the effort and energy of each sales person. Attitude, the proverbial "thick skin", relentless high-achievement drive and energy are typical characteristics of commission-based sales people.

THE FORMULA AND ITS COMPONENTS

There is no formula for commissions. Senior management set specific targets for revenues, profits or units sold during the annual business budgeting and planning cycle. These targets are divided into smaller goals across the sales team, weighted according to the company's needs, the size of each sales person's territory, the dynamics of the market and the "stretch" goals set by sales management to challenge each sales person to improve their performance over the preceding year. The challenge here is choosing a compensation system that is aligned with company objectives.

WHERE'S THE DATA?

Figures for revenues, profits and units are unique to each company. The data is based on financial performance over a designated period or periods. Sales management review the growth rates in recent years and may decide to use the previous year's growth rate for the current planning year's projections. Often, any expected departures (either up or down) from recent growth rates are factored into management's planning and goal setting to arrive at this final projection.

Individual targets are set by management for each sales rep, usually in consultation with them, and based on past performance, often with the addition of a "stretch" goal above and beyond the individual's regular performance. Commission percentages are decided by sales management, using company and/or industry practices as a guideline.

CALCULATING IT

Since there is no formula, there is no calculation. However, it is helpful to visualize the sales process using a familiar tool: the product lifecycle "S-curve", as shown in Figure 17.1 below. Each product tends to follow a multi-stage development and growth sequence. This sequence describes how products grow over time. Most business literature on this topic identifies the stages as: introduction, growth, maturity and decline. The product lifecycle is not limited to products, however. It is a useful mechanism to describe a company's evolution, marketing stages and even changing customer dynamics. In the early stages (particularly the introduction stage) sales people are working hard to attract new customers.

Figure 17.1   The product lifecycle "S-curve"

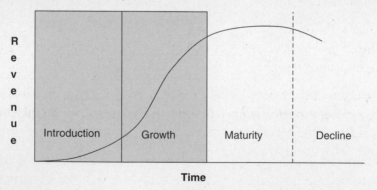

Convincing customers to buy new products is time-consuming and hard work, even if the company is already established. Sales people thrive on success and expect to be rewarded for their efforts. Straight commission rewards the sales person's specific achievements.

WHAT IT MEANS AND POTENTIAL CHALLENGES

Sales management need to be clear about how commissions are determined. Commissions paid at the close of sale will likely be different (and higher, costing the company more) than those paid when the final product is delivered because there may be additional costs (post-sale discounts, payment terms) that can erode the initial price agreed upon with the customer.

There are additional pros and cons to be considered in determining whether to pay sales staff solely on a commission basis:

PROS

- Straight commission inspires rapid growth since sales people are motivated to find new customers because the alternative is having no income.

- Straight commission will attract sales people with high ambition and aggressiveness.

- Commission-sales people are risk takers and expect to be compensated for their hard work. They thrive on rewards and, conceivably, commissions have unlimited potential — as long as the sales person keeps finding new customers, he or she will earn more money.

- Commission-sales people are highly individualistic and need little direction. This allows management to focus more on strategic and operational issues.

- Straight commission can keep costs lower during a downturn since less compensation is paid when there are fewer or smaller customer orders.

- Commissions are correlated with goals, so sales management can set specific quantitative targets against which performance can be easily measured.

- Commission-sales people in many companies do not receive benefits (medical, dental, life insurance, profit sharing), thus reducing employee expenses.

CONS

- While commissions can be as simple as a straight percentage of total sales, companies will often vary commission percentages based on strategic objectives and product position needs. This can lead to a complex compensation plan that is challenging to track and administer accurately.

- Commission-sales people may be more of a hired gun than a team player, moving jobs, companies or industries as commissions change.

- Commission-sales people are less likely to perform non-sales tasks and may be unwilling to do basic administrative record keeping.

References

Cron, W. L., T. E. DeCarlo and D. J. Palrymple. *Sales Management*, John Wiley & Sons, Inc., 2004: p. 501.

Davis, J. *Measuring Marketing: 103 Key Metrics Every Marketer Needs*, John Wiley & Sons (Asia) Pte Ltd., 2007.

Doyle, C. *Collins Internet-Linked Dictionary of Marketing*, Harper Collins, 2003, 2006: p. 72.

http://www.eridlc.com/onlinetextbook/index.cfm?fuseaction=textbook.chpt19

http://www.marketingpower.com/mg-dictionary.php?Searched=1&   SearchFor= straight%20commission%20plan

18 Profit–Based Commission

THE DEFINITION

A profit-based commission rewards the sales person for generating sales at or above a specific profit level. Volume selling as a sales approach (on which straight commission is based) quickly disappears as a consequence of being rewarded for specific profit achievements (assuming the sales person wishes to continue earning a living). As with any business, commission percentages will be based on each company's unique needs and performance objectives.

THE FORMULA AND ITS COMPONENTS

There is no formula for profit-based commissions.

WHERE'S THE DATA?

The data used by sales management originates from previous company history with the product's sales and selling price, as well as the expectations for improved profit performance in the coming business cycle. Company management may decide that the low-price-driven market-share gains from the volume-based commission selling in Magic Number 17 are not sustainable, or investors may be applying pressure on company management to demonstrate improved profitability. In either case, the data used to determine the need for increased profitability comes from a combination of past performance, competitors' profits for similar products, industry standards, and customer perceptions. Senior management's decision results from an informal mix of objective and subjective factors that guide, rather than dictate, desired profit levels.

CALCULATING IT

Straight-commission sales as discussed in Magic Number 17 serve to increase sales volume and market share. Over time, management will want to shift to rewards for achieving specific profit levels on each sale. This will be particularly true as a company makes the transition from rapid growth (often generated by aggressive volume selling to gain share) to a greater emphasis on higher margins on each sale, essentially a progression into the mature stage of the product lifecycle "S-curve" that we looked at in Magic Number 17. This occurs as competitors move into the market after seeing the success earned by current players, leading to a decline in prices in their efforts to steal share. Companies are forced to look for ways to improve their profitability, through a combination of cost controls, value-added changes to the product and a sales approach that motivates the sales person to sell differently if they are to earn commissions.

Figure 18.1   The product lifecycle "S-curve": Entering Maturity

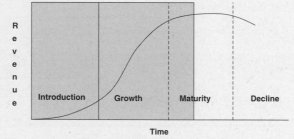

WHAT IT MEANS AND POTENTIAL CHALLENGES

Sales people will alter their behavior when the objectives are clear and they are rewarded for doing so. Sales management can mandate a flat profit level across all products, or set specific profit levels to be achieved on each product individually. The challenge in tracking profit-based commissions is enabling the sales person to have access to cost information so they can determine the kind of selling required to ensure that the overall profit objective is achieved. Without cost information, the sales person will struggle in adapting final prices to each customer's unique needs.

References

Cron, W. L., T. E. DeCarlo and D. J. Palrymple, *Sales Management*, John Wiley & Sons, Inc., 2004: pp. 507–509.

Davis, J. *Measuring Marketing: 103 Key Metrics Every Marketer Needs,* John Wiley & Sons (Asia) Pte Ltd., 2007.

Straight Salary

THE DEFINITION

A straight salary is a wage payment set at a fixed amount for a specific period of time.

THE FORMULA AND ITS COMPONENTS

There is no formula for straight salary.

WHERE'S THE DATA?

Sales management will base salary decisions on their company's compensation guidelines. More companies are developing salary grades for different jobs and experience levels, so the amount paid to new sales people will correspond with their experience and job responsibilities. Industry comparisons are easily found on the Internet, through market research reports, trade journals and in-house salary surveys.

CALCULATING IT

As businesses grow, so does the complexity of their product lines and the markets they serve. Products are very likely to be at different points along the classic product lifecycle "S-curve" discussed in Magic Number 17. Each stage's unique dynamics require different marketing approaches to meet the needs of customers, which are changing throughout this cycle.

While aggressive selling approaches are useful for attracting customers in the introduction and growth stages (and incentive-laden compensation schemes support this type of selling), customers in the maturity stage are

Figure 19.1   The product lifecycle "S-curve": in maturity

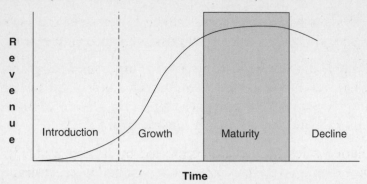

unlikely to respond favorably to sales tactics employed in these earlier stages. Customers in the maturity stage are more devoted and want their loyalty rewarded through better understanding of their needs and more personal communication. Often, customers in the maturity stage are handled by a separate account-management team, with different skills from the more aggressive early-stage sales team. Consequently, the account manager's compensation should reward a proven ability to manage the customer relationship over the long term, and a straight salary is a more useful method to accomplish this.

As we have seen in earlier Magic Numbers, incentive-based plans motivate sales people to seek only the best customers. But sales management may seek complete coverage of all potential customers in a territory, rather than just the top ones. Straight salary is a viable compensation approach to satisfy this need as well.

What It Means and Potential Challenges

Sales compensation will vary, depending on the stage of the lifecycle for the company, its products and its customers, with each requiring a different sales approach. Straight salary is particularly useful when the company's intent is to nurture relationships with its most loyal customers. Sales management sets targets for the sales force in the annual sales plan. Straight salary is useful when the targets are more qualitative ("keep the customer happy") than quantitative ("increase volume by 15%") because the individual's impact on sales volume is harder to measure and, therefore, does not lend itself to commission-based rewards.

There are additional pros and cons to be considered in deciding on straight salary as a compensation scheme.

PROS

- Customers will expect service to be better, since the salaried sales person is focused on the relationship rather than the next sale.

- Straight-salary systems can serve to attract sales people with better service and relationship-development skills. (More aggressive sales people who prefer higher-risk/higher-reward commission systems will find straight salary unattractive.)

- Salaried sales people are comforted by having a steady income, since their next paycheck is not dependent on generating revenues from new customers (assuming a downturn does not lead to their termination or forced salary reductions).

- Salaried sales people are compensated more like non-sales management and, therefore, will likely be more willing to perform non-sales activities.

- Straight salary is easier for business and financial-planning purposes since there is less complexity in the compensation structure. Sales cycles can be volatile and incentive-laden compensation plans can create uneven cash-flow needs. Straight salary helps management keep expenses at a more constant level, with fewer surprises.

CONS

- Salary expense remains constant even when sales levels decline, reducing margins more than a commission-based sales person's compensation.

- Salaried sales people may be less motivated than their incentive-based counterparts, who are driven to make the next sale. Sales management's challenge is to motivate salaried sales people to keep loyal customers happy, even though the rewards are less tangible. Sales management must clearly describe to each salaried sales person how their role contributes to customer success.

- Performance standards, especially the more qualitative and intangible objectives, must be clearly articulated to the salaried sales people. This is not easy because of the imprecision of measuring behavior and will perhaps require sales management to be more directly involved with their field sales representatives.

Since we have examined both straight commission and straight salary in the last two chapters, let's compare the compensation plans of each. The following figure[1] assumes a commission rate of 10% as opposed to a straight salary of $40,000.

Figure 19.2   Straight commission vs straight salary: a comparison

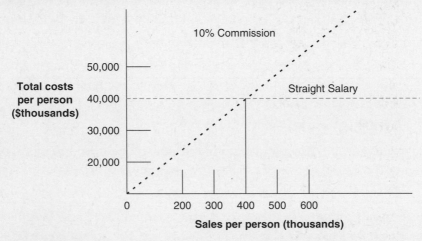

The commission costs the company less than the salary until a certain sales level per person is achieved — $400,000 in this example. Comparing this result to the example of the classic S-curve — whereby it was asserted that a more aggressive sales approach is often needed in the introduction and growth stages, and a more service-oriented account-management approach is needed in the maturity stage — we see that a similar result occurs. As sales grow in the figure above, the company is moving from the earlier stages toward maturity, where a straight salary becomes more cost effective.

Endnote

[1]Cron, W. L., T. E. DeCarlo and D. J. Palrymple, *Sales Management*, John Wiley & Sons, Inc., 2004: p.502.

Additional References

Davis, J. *Measuring Marketing: 103 Key Metrics Every Marketer Needs,* John Wiley & Sons (Asia) Pte Ltd., 2007.
Cron, et al., op.cit.
http://www.marketingpower.com/mg-dictionary-view3054.php
http://www.eridlc.com/onlinetextbook/index.cfm?fuseaction=textbook.chpt19
http://www.econ.jku.at/Winter/lazear/Lecture5.pdf

20 Salary Plus Commission or Bonus

THE DEFINITION

Salary plus commission or bonus is compensation based on a combination of fixed payments and variable rewards.

THE FORMULA AND ITS COMPONENTS

There is no set formula for this metric.

WHERE'S THE DATA?

As we have seen with Magic Numbers 17–19 (and will also see with Numbers 21–23), compensation will be based on the company's own pay scales, with influence from industry pay standards providing guidance as well.

CALCULATING IT[1]

As discussed in Magic Number 19, an important disadvantage of straight-salary compensation is the lack of reward for extraordinary performance. Sales people on straight salary are unlikely to be motivated to achieve specific targets since there is no corresponding reward. Sales management may decide to set more specific goals, and will need a compensation plan that rewards achievement accordingly. As a company grows and matures, the number of products increases, as does the number of customers and markets served. Straight commission is no longer adequate to address the competing strategic objectives of the company and its evolving customer base. A more diverse sales-compensation plan may be needed to address the different demands of each product at each stage.

Salary plus commission or bonus offers management an important tool to motivate behavior, since rewards are tied to accomplishments beyond the basic management expectations covered by straight salary. Salary plus commission and salary plus bonus are discussed individually below, along with the impact of each on decision-making processes.

Salary Plus Commission (SPC)

The logic behind salary plus commission is simply to help sales management motivate sales people, particularly B2B sellers involved in lengthy sales cycles, to achieve specific targets by paying them a commission if the goal is reached. B2B sales people receive salary as a base level of income to compensate for the longer time between each sale. If and when the sale occurs, a commission is paid, although this is generally smaller than a straight commission. This affords management a fair amount of flexibility in that they can set different commission percentages based on the importance of the strategic need.

For example, let's look at an enterprise-software company selling a range of software applications in three categories: databases, financial applications and sales-force automation. Its sales people receive a base salary, which helps offset income declines during business down cycles. The company's management decides that the performance of its sales-force automation business can be improved, so it sets a commission of 5% for monthly sales increases up to $100,000. If a sales person sells an additional $100,001 to $124,999, then the commission increases to 7.5% on those sales in this range. And if the target is exceeded by more than $125,000, then the sales person receives a 10% commission for any sales over that amount.

WHAT IT MEANS AND POTENTIAL CHALLENGES[2]

PROS

- SPC can help a company achieve important, short-term goals (sell more soft candy to retail accounts, for example).

- SPC can improve the performance of specific products or services since sales people will be rewarded for focusing their effort on the selected areas of need.

- Commissions paid regularly are a great source of motivation because the sales person gets almost immediate financial benefit as well as recognition for achievement.

CONS

- Similar to straight-commission sales, SPC can become complex, particularly with large product lines.

- Commissions are like marketing promotions and can be expensive in the short term since the company will pay out more in additional financial reward as more sales are generated. It raises the strategic question of whether there is a long-term benefit, such as increased customer loyalty, or if the commission incentive merely spikes revenue only for the length of the program.

- Commissions tend to reward volume at the expense of profits, so they should be designed carefully.

Salary Plus Bonus (SPB)

SPB programs are typically structured around quotas, specific targets derived from company goals. Whereas commissions may be related to individual products and individual sales, quotas are more often tied to growth objectives for customers (both new customers and/or share of customer increases) or total product sales (units or dollars). If the quotas are achieved, then a bonus is paid on a quarterly, semi-annual or annual basis.

For example, let's look at the enterprise-software company again. The company's management decides to increase market share in the next year, as measured by units sold. Furthermore, management determines that it wants to grow its market share in the banking sector by 3%. Sales management would establish quotas for each rep, based on their territory, with the aggregate total quotas equaling or exceeding the 3% market-share improvement goal. If sales reps meet their quota, which is known as "achieving quota", they then receive a bonus at the end of the pay period. Many companies will reward for performances that exceed quota, increasing the bonus as the situation warrants.

WHAT IT MEANS AND POTENTIAL CHALLENGES[3]

PROS

- SPB helps align a sales person's efforts with longer-term company strategic objectives (to, say, increase market share by 3% this year; increase profits per sale by 5%).

- SPB may inspire a more complete, business-oriented approach since rewards will be based on a combination of sales, profits and customer growth, as opposed to the one-sided volume emphasis of commission compensation.

- SPB rewards longer-term behavior, so it can encourage better sales force retention.

- SPB provides a more controlled outflow of funds than commission-based sales since bonuses are usually paid on an annual basis, rather than the sale-by-sale basis of commissions. This provides more predictable and stable financial control.

CONS

- Companies usually allocate a finite pool of money for bonuses, and a percentage-payout range that limits rewards. A percentage-payout range is issued by senior management, setting limits on bonuses, based on performance. For example, the range might be 3% to 6%, with top performers earning 6%. In this situation, top-performing sales people may be insufficiently rewarded for extraordinary achievement. Therefore, the company risks losing its best talent while retaining average or even poor performers.

- Bonuses are less precise. Whereas a commission is tied directly to an increase in sales, it is harder to correlate a bonus payout to the more complete business approach of revenues, profits and customer growth.

- Bonuses are paid less often than commissions. Since sales people thrive on reward, the longer wait to receive a bonus may be demotivating.

Endnotes

[1] Adapted from the article, "Sales Compensation: Creating Performance Clarity" by John F. Tallitsch, Managing Director for TOPMARK LLC http://www.ezinearticles.com/?Sales-Compensation:-Creating-Performance-Clarity&id=151492

[2] Adapted from: Cron, W. L., T. E. DeCarlo and D. J. Palrymple, *Sales Management*. John Wiley & Sons, Inc., 2004: pp. 502–503.

[3] Ibid pp. 503–504.

Additional References

Davis, J. *Measuring Marketing: 103 Key Metrics Every Marketer Needs,* John Wiley & Sons (Asia) Pte Ltd., 2007.

http://waternet.com/article.asp?IndexID=6634018

21 Salary Plus Commission and Bonus

THE DEFINITION[1]

Salary plus commission and bonus is compensation based on a combination of fixed payments and bonus rewards.

Salary plus commission and bonus allows management to compensate sales people with a steady salary plus commissions to inspire individual performance behaviors and bonuses, usually based on the achievement of company performance milestones. Alternatively, management may choose to vary the structure to a combination of salary, commissions for accomplishing specific individual and team goals, and bonuses paid annually for company performance and customer-satisfaction scores.

THE FORMULA AND ITS COMPONENTS

There is no formula for this metric.

WHERE'S THE DATA?

Compensation is based on the company's own pay scales. Data on industry pay standards offers guidance as well.

CALCULATING IT

In Magic Number 20, we discussed the value of a more sophisticated sales compensation plan that gives sales management the choice of adding a commission or bonus to base salary. Many companies, particularly large multi-nationals, operate in multiple environments,

Figure 21.1   Using the "S-curve" in determining sales compensation.

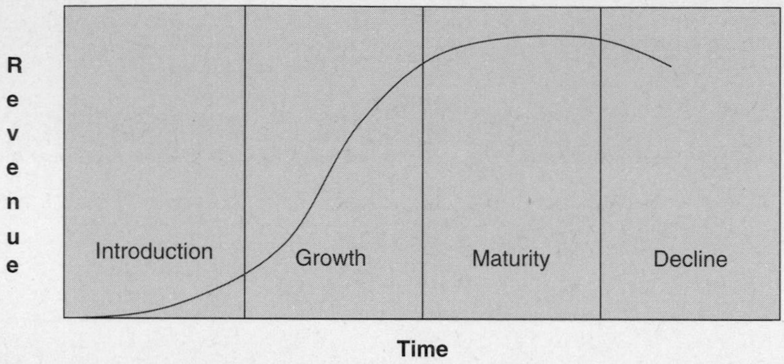

each at different stages of market development and with correspondingly varied financial performance objectives. If this is the case, sales management can offer compensation that combines salary, commission and bonus to effectively target the varied business environments (and their sales requirements) in which they operate.

WHAT IT MEANS AND POTENTIAL CHALLENGES

The advantages to commissions and bonuses were enumerated in depth in Magic Number 20. The most attractive element is the maximum flexibility that they afford to sales management in structuring rewards to achieve multiple corporate objectives. They also allow the field sales person to adopt a sales approach best suited to their abilities. Conversely, the risk is that companies with multiple products, customers and markets also have varied, and often quite complex, performance objectives, making this type of compensation challenging for management to administer and for sales people to understand. An unfortunate side-effect may be a sub-optimal effort by the sales person who, instead of trying to master the complexity of the compensation plan to maximize rewards, opts instead to pursue a "low-hanging fruit" approach to sales — working on those goals that involve the least hassle for themselves, and sacrificing some of the company's overall objectives.

Endnote

[1] Adapted from: Cron, W. L., T. E. DeCarlo and D. J. Palrymple, *Sales Management*, John Wiley & Sons, Inc., 2004: pp. 504–505.

Additional Reference

Davis, J. *Measuring Marketing: 103 Key Metrics Every Marketer Needs,* John Wiley & Sons (Asia) Pte Ltd., 2007.

22

Commission Plus Bonus

The Definition[1]

Commission plus bonus describes compensation that uses only variable payments. No salary is involved.

The Formula and Its Components

There is no formula for this metric.

Where's the Data?

As with Magic Numbers 17–21, commission and bonus levels are established by sales management using internal criteria. Industry data on comparable variable pay amounts can serve as an external guideline, helping sales management ensure their compensation practices are competitive.

Calculating It

Companies with a sales force composed of mostly contracted third-party (independent) sales reps, such as real-estate firms or industries that rely on part-time help, do not want the overhead expense of fixed salaries. Yet these companies still need to attract and reward sales people. Brokerage firms, multi-level marketing companies and even high-tech start-ups often utilize a commission-plus-bonus compensation package as it can apply to any stage in the product lifecycle.

Figure 22.1   Using the "S-curve" in determining sales compensaton (II)

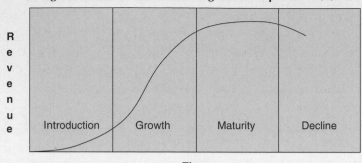

WHAT IT MEANS AND POTENTIAL CHALLENGES

An advantage to the company is the elimination of fixed salary expenses that pay even if the sales person does not perform. Commission plus bonus also enables the company to compensate sales people only when they make a sale, so the reward is effectively funded from the proceeds arising from the sale to the customer. Commission-based rewards inspire sales people because rewards are tied directly and immediately to accomplishment. The disadvantage is that sales people may take unnecessary risks to earn rewards, including employing overly aggressive sales techniques that may eventually serve to undermine, rather than develop, customer relationships.

The bonus component, as discussed in Magic Numbers 20–21, motivates a longer-term behavior by paying the reward after a specific period of time, usually for company, division or team goals that have been achieved. If the longer-term goals are not met, then the bonus is not paid and the sales person is paid on commission-based sales alone.

Like straight commission (Magic Number 17), this is a Darwinian approach. It has the benefit to the company of reducing expenses since no salaries are paid, but it can also create cash-flow volatility since commissions are paid as sales come in. To survive, the sales person must sell. To thrive, the sales person must sell and achieve certain longer-term goals that are often tied to overall company performance. Commission plus bonus attracts a specific kind of sales person, one who is highly independent and self-sufficient, and may also not enjoy structured reporting relationships. In most companies, non-salaried people usually do not receive benefits (Starbucks being a rare exception), so the sales people are responsible for arranging their own medical and other insurance needs, which are paid out of their earnings. These sales people tend to be entrepreneurial and find the risks exhilarating because the rewards, if they come, can be high. If an organization simply seeks aggressive sales growth, then this approach can work well. But if the company seeks more loyalty from its sales team, then this form of compensation will not attract the right talent.

Endnote

[1] Adapted from: Cron, W. L., T. E. DeCarlo and D. J. Palrymple, *Sales Management*, John Wiley & Sons, Inc., 2004: p. 505.

Additional Reference

Davis, J. *Measuring Marketing: 103 Key Metrics Every Marketer Needs,* John Wiley & Sons (Asia) Pte Ltd., 2007.

23 Team–Selling Compensation

The Definition

Team-selling compensation is variable compensation paid upon the achievement of a team goal.

The Formula and Its Components

Once again, there is no specific formula for this metric. Sales management are responsible for setting relevant team targets and creating an environment conducive to coordinated and successful cooperative selling by all sales representatives.

Where's the Data?

Sales management will have their own internal benchmarks for developing a practical team-selling compensation plan. As with other compensation plans discussed in earlier Magic Numbers, compensation guidelines will be based on a combination of the company's internal performance targets and industry pay standards for equivalent work.

Calculating it

Companies with a large sales force will find that sales territories often overlap. Customer operations may be spread across multiple sales territories, for example. Or, a customer may seek a product represented by another sales person in a different market. Sales management need a way to motivate the sales people involved to coordinate their expertise for the benefit of the customer and to close the sale.

Figure 23.1   Using the "S-curve" in determining sales compensation (III)

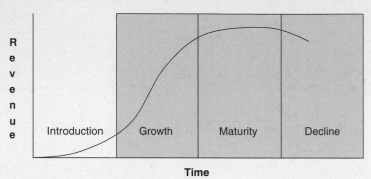

Team selling is unlikely to be needed at the introduction stage of the product lifecycle since, as a matter of survival, the company is emphasizing sales to as many customers as possible. Team selling would pull valuable resources from multiple segments and customers to concentrate on a few, reducing the odds of succeeding past this early stage. Even in the growth stage, team selling is less likely because the company is still building its customer base, solidifying its market-share gains and trying to satisfy growing demand for its initial group of products.

The shift into late growth and maturity, and perhaps even decline, is when team selling may be necessary, as the company looks toward new ways to satisfy existing customers and expands its product and solution offering. The company's customers have been growing as well, with changing needs and increasingly dispersed operations, so the momentum toward overlapping territories and combined sales efforts will grow as well.

A team-selling compensation program can address this issue. Two or more sales people (it is conceivable that a selling team may contain non-sales people, particularly with industrial and high-tech businesses) combine efforts to maximize a sale, improve the financial outcome for their company and deliver a solution that could not have been completed in the absence of the team.

Structuring such compensation plans can be complex. Sales management should develop clear goals that are consistent with their company's strategic objectives, paying rewards only when those goals are achieved through a coordinated team effort. When developing an account-specific compensation plan, sales management should be clear on how the team is to perform, from customer interactions to ongoing internal progress reporting. Mapping team members and their respective roles (such as identifying who is the lead sales person, who the technical sales specialist is, who is responsible for the long-term account management, and who is responsible for internal communication with other company departments) and the roles of their counterparts on the buying team is a key component of the team-compensation plan. Alternatively, team-selling reward systems do not have to be account-specific. Territory or field-office goals (such as improvements in market share, margin performance, or share of customer wallet) can also serve as viable team-oriented targets whereby the reward is paid only if the entire team succeeds in attaining a territory goal. Individual sales representatives may have outstanding performances, but unless the overall team goal is achieved as well, no compensation is paid.

David Steitz, president of Characters Inc., a multimillion-dollar computer type-setting business in Houston, uses the team sales and planning approach to win over clients during particularly tough presentations.

"[We once] had a large catalog to do for a customer, and we had never dealt with them before. So we developed a team of six people in our company from various disciplines," says Steitz. "The team included myself, the sales representative from my company, the customer service rep, the technical computer specialist, the trainer, and the software specialist meeting with our client."

The sales rep and Steitz were only there to facilitate the discussion and to introduce the other team members. During the sales presentation, which was conducted more like a planning session than a sales meeting, each team member gave a presentation explaining his or her role in the project, as if they were already doing the job.

"I wish I could tell you that this was all done intentionally, but it just happened that way," Steitz says. "My other team members were not sales people — they were just folks who do the work and do it well. This fact came across brilliantly, and we ended up going from what was supposed to be a typical sales presentation, to a planning meeting, to scheduling with the prospects when we could actually start the project. It was magical."

Source: Kennedy, D. "Dream Teams – Team Buying and Selling", *Entrepreneur Magazine*, September 1997.

WHAT IT MEANS AND POTENTIAL CHALLENGES

The decision to create a team-selling plan presents sales management with a challenge since sales people are predisposed toward individual achievement. The structure of the compensation plan must be able to satisfy the needs of multiple parties: the individuals, the team and, most importantly, the customer.

A sales manager will want to weigh the opportunity costs of supporting a team for the benefit of one customer against those of continuing independent selling by each sales person. Sales management need to have a clear understanding of what is expected in each of the following areas:

- **Team work:** Who will be on the team? How is the team's work to be allocated? Is this designed to enhance collaboration for the long term?

- **Objectives:** Is the proposed team satisfying a one-time need, or is it part of a more significant company restructuring to encourage more cohesive sales objectives? Is the company's customer base changing, requiring expansion of the team-selling effort and a move away from individual achievement? How will productivity be measured? How will financial success be measured — through improved revenues, profits or units sold? Will there be an emphasis on different products? How will this affect recruiting?

- **Individual performance:** How will individual contribution to the team be evaluated?

- **Managerial support:** Will management support the team's efforts? Will management support team bonuses? How will management review performance?

- **Reward fairness:** Can contribution imbalances be addressed fairly? How is reward size determined — by team or by individual? Will the bonus sufficiently reward the team effort?

- **Employee input:** How much input will each team member have toward the group effort? Will individual inputs be considered by management before the team plan is completed? Will team members have input on quality issues?

References

Adapted from: Cron, W. L., T. E. DeCarlo and D. J. Palrymple, *Sales Management,* John Wiley & Sons, Inc., 2004: p. 507.

Davis, J. *Measuring Marketing: 103 Key Metrics Every Marketer Needs,* John Wiley & Sons (Asia) Pte Ltd., 2007.

http://www.coba.unt.edu/MGMT/Johnson/Courses/366.17.Gainsharing

http://www.findarticles.com/p/articles/mimDDTT/is_n9_v25/ai_19892331

24

Segment Profitability[1]

THE DEFINITION

Segment profitability measures whether a segment that is attractive from a revenue standpoint will also be profitable. Sales and marketing management must have a clear sense of their company's strategic opportunities within the overall market, and STP (segmentation, targeting and positioning) is the tool most frequently used. STP, specifically segmentation, breaks the market into smaller groups of customers who share common characteristics and/or have similar needs so that the marketing effort can be tailored to those specific groups. The company then targets those segments that are best addressed by its core competencies and capabilities. As products gain favor and the business grows, marketers need to pay close attention to the target segment's profitability, and not just the revenues it generates.

THE FORMULAS AND THEIR COMPONENTS

Three formulas are used, each of which contributes to describing the overall understanding and attractiveness of the market segment in question.

1.

$$C_{nm} = \{D_s \times S_s \times (P_{pu} \times M)\} - E_m$$

Where

C_{nm} = net marketing contribution

D_s = segment demand

S_s = segment share
P_{pu} = price per unit
M = percentage margin
E_m = marketing expense

2.

$$\text{Marketing ROS} = \frac{C_{nm}}{S} \times 100\%$$

Where

Marketing ROS = marketing return on sales
C_{nm} = net marketing contribution
S = sales

3.

$$\text{ROI} = \frac{C_{nm}}{E_m} \times 100\%$$

Where

ROI = return on investment
C_{nm} = net marketing contribution
E_m = marketing expense

WHERE'S THE DATA?

Segment-demand and segment-share statistics are gathered through market research. Primary research would be conducted or commissioned directly by the marketing and/or sales departments to study the market. Most industries have trade journals that publish annual statistics. General business magazines often cite such statistics as well. The net marketing contribution, margin percentages, marketing expenses and price per unit are all found in the detailed account records for each customer, which are summarized in the income statement. Both the detailed account records and income statement are found in the finance department. The sales and marketing plans and related programs may also list pricing information, although this is likely to be in a more hypothetical "ideal world" stage and not in the actual market data.

CALCULATING IT

Let's look at the following hypothetical example. Euro Bike is based in Europe and manufactures bicycles. We will further assume that demand for bicycles across the European continent is three million units per year. Euro Bike has been in this market for 20 years and has developed a strong reputation for reliable and affordable bicycles targeted at the entry-level consumer. The company has a 25% market share in what is otherwise a fragmented industry. Euro Bike's products are built of quality parts but have few extra features, thus selling for $50. By contrast, premium bikes with composite materials, sophisticated gear technology and state-of-the-art shock absorbers sell for as much as $3,500. Bicycle manufacturing is expensive because of the number of parts that are put together by hand. Euro Bike's main facilities are located in Estonia, where wages are lower. Consequently, Euro Bike's costs are slightly more manageable than most competitors' in the industry, which helps it maintain 15% margins. It focuses its marketing efforts on point-of-purchase displays and minor promotional giveaways such as seat covers and reflectors. Total sales are $37,500,000. Its total marketing expenses are 10% of sales.

These figures are plugged directly into the formulas:

$$C_{nm} = \{D_s \times S_s \times (P_{pu} \times M)\} - E_m$$
$$= \{3,000,000 \times 25\% \times (50 \times 15\%)\} - \$3,750,000$$
$$= \$1,875,000$$

This means that Euro Bike's efforts to target the entry-level bike buyer have a net marketing contribution of $1,875,000.

Now, let's bring in the other two formulas to fully measure the attractiveness of this segment:

$$ROS = \frac{C_{nm}}{S} \times 100\%$$

$$ROS = \frac{\$1,875,000}{\$37,500,000} \times 100\%$$

$$= 5\%$$

$$ROI = \frac{C_{nm}}{E_m} \times 100\%$$

$$ROI = \frac{\$1,875,000}{\$3,750,000} \times 100\%$$

$$= 50\%$$

Euro Bike's return on sales is 5% and its return on investment is 50%. While these results may be consistent with the bicycle industry overall, Euro Bike would have to compare its figures with those of specific competitors in the sub-segment of entry-level bicycles to help determine if this is a good performance. Of course, the company should have its own internal performance expectations as well. Assuming its industry research suggests comparable performance and its internal performance targets are met, then Euro Bike ought to be pleased.

Segment-demand and segment-share statistics are gathered through market research, both primary (conducted or commissioned directly by a company's marketing management to study the market), and secondary (trade journals that publish annual statistics, and general business magazines such as *BusinessWeek, The Economist and Fortune Magazine*). The net marketing contribution, margin percentages, marketing expenses and price per unit are all found in the company's detailed account records for each customer, which are most likely summarized in the income statement. The marketing plan and programs may also list pricing information, although this is likely to be in a more hypothetical "ideal world" stage and not in the actual market data.

WHAT IT MEANS AND POTENTIAL CHALLENGES

The decision to target a particular segment is influenced by whether the segment has the potential to achieve a specific or desired level of profitability. The first formula, net marketing contribution, helps sales and marketing management understand a given segment's profit potential and, therefore, its general attractiveness as a business opportunity. Marketing ROS describes the return on total sales, which is dependent on knowing the net marketing contribution. It is an important indicator of the efficiency of the company's operations. A lower marketing ROS signals either a decrease in pricing or an increase in expenses. This helps managers understand whether or not the return is attractive from the perspective of total sales generated, and is an indicator of the effectiveness of the sales effort. Finally, marketing ROI measures the total return on the marketing investment, indicating whether the expenditures on marketing are yielding maximum results.

Segment profitability is a useful method to assess the attractiveness of specific audiences being targeted and the resulting success from customer-development efforts. It can help companies understand how different components of their marketing investments affect profitability, which can guide sales and marketing decisions for the future. Each segment, however, is likely to be unique and success (or failure) in one does not guarantee a similar performance in another. Marketers and field-sales representatives need to use the various marketing tools at their disposal to adjust the value proposition, ensuring that they are fine-tuning their efforts based on the characteristics of a given segment. This is one of the central challenges in the execution of sales and marketing programs and it is a reason why marketing results can be perceived as disappointing when reviewed by CFOs and CEOs. Marketers may implement a common campaign across multiple segments and sales may implement the program consistently, yet only one segment may respond favorably. Consequently, the overall sales and marketing effort looks wrong; yet the useful lesson is the response of the segment that found the proposition attractive (and, of course, the sales and marketing managers now know the tactics that do not work with the other segments). Marketers must develop their budgets and programs in cooperation with sales management. Both sales and marketing should be in clear agreement on the different programs required to reach each audience BEFORE going to market, so that the power of marketing can be fully realized. In consumer-products companies, marketers often pre-test new products and marketing campaigns in niche markets, or even with focus groups, to gain a better understanding of the potential attractiveness of the offering. Positive test results provide sales management with credible evidence to present to target customers about the attractiveness of the offerings.

Furthermore, products face different lifecycle stages in different markets, depending on the newness of the product, the maturity of the market, or even geographic issues, thus requiring different marketing approaches to reach satisfactory performance levels.

Segment profitability is important in both the planning and review stages of the marketing-planning effort. Sales and marketing managers must justify their overall budgets and proposed expenditures, and segment profitability is a relevant measure in this effort. It is also a practical tool in reviewing the success of a company's total marketing activities that are directed toward a specific segment since sales and marketing management can compare actual performance to expectations from the start of the planning period.

Endnote

[1] Adapted from: Best, R. J. *Market-Based Management: Strategies for Growing Customer Value and Profitability*, Upper Saddle River, New Jersey: Pearson Education Inc., 2005: pp. 145–147.

Additional References

Davis, J. *Magic Numbers for Consumer Marketing,* John Wiley & Sons, 2005: pp. 145–150.

Davis, J. *Measuring Marketing: 103 Key Metrics Every Marketer Needs,* John Wiley & Sons (Asia) Pte Ltd., 2007.

Wilson, R. M. S. and C. Gilliagan, *Strategic Marketing Management: Planning Implementation and Control,* Elsevier Butterworth-Heinemann, 2005: pp. 318–320.

Share of Customer

THE DEFINITION

Share of customer describes a company's sales to a customer as a percentage of the customer's total purchases for products of that type. It is also known as "share of the customer's wallet".

THE FORMULA AND ITS COMPONENTS

Conceptually, share of customer is similar to market share, except that market share is sales (units or dollars) as a percentage of total sales of all companies for a given product and/or market.

The formula is:

$$S_i = \frac{S_{it}}{Mt_t} \times 100$$

Where

S_i = share of customer i (in percentage terms)
S_{it} = sales to customer i in time t (in units or dollars)
Mt_t = sum of all customer spending in time t (in units or dollars)

WHERE'S THE DATA?

Data for sales is found in the company's financial statements. Industry data from market-research firms, industry surveys, competitive intelligence from consultancies and even Wall Street industry reports are likely to have the information required to assess all customer spending. Share-of-customer information is likely to be kept in the reports of those who work closest with customers — field sales and marketing. Managers in these functions have deep knowledge of their customers and direct account responsibility, which is often a combination of quantitative data and qualitative insights about the unique profiles of each customer. Top-performing sales people are quite familiar with the resources and spending patterns of their customers. However, this information is rarely stored in formal accounting or financial reports since these reports are designed to review performance in aggregate and not at the individual-customer level. Furthermore, the information sales people have about their customer accounts includes subjective insights, based on their personal experiences and observations from direct interactions. Most of this information is not useful for formal accounting and financial tracking purposes, yet it is vital to a sales person's knowledge of individual customer accounts.

CALCULATING IT

To illustrate, if a customer has $1 million to spend on a given type of product, and a company's sales to that particular customer total $100,000, then the company has a 10% share of customer, as follows:

$$S = \frac{\$100,000}{\$1,000,000} \times 100$$

$$= 10\%$$

Conversely, of course, if that customer buys $900,000 of the product from the company, then the share of customer is 90%.

The athletic-footwear industry, for example, uses share of customer as one of the measures for evaluating the many retail buyers with which they work. Buyers from large retail sporting goods and footwear chains have budgets comprising planned purchases and units that have already been ordered. The difference between these two is called "open to buy" dollars, which is the remaining money a buyer has available to spend on footwear products. A footwear-sales representative who knows the retail buyer well will also know the amount of open-to-buy dollars that are uncommitted. Persuading the retail buyer to allocate most, or all, of their remaining budget toward purchases of the sales rep's footwear products will increase the company's share of customer.

WHAT IT MEANS AND POTENTIAL CHALLENGES

Measuring sales success with customers extends beyond acquiring customers and growing market share to include increasing the company's share of each acquired customer's business. Share of customer is a useful guide for sales management in assessing their success at persuading a customer to purchase a larger share of their products than those of the competition. Share of customer is also a valuable measure for assessing the performance of individual sales representatives since it is a partial indicator of how successful they are in developing their customer relationships.

Share-of-customer results can be a driver of customer-relationship programs designed to improve loyalty, yet they are also an early indicator of product problems if there is a decline in average per-customer purchases over time or if the customer increases purchases of a competitor's products. However, sales and marketing management must also be aware that individual customers are subject to business cycles that will undoubtedly influence purchase decisions. Therefore, sales and marketing should work closely together since the field-sales organization works with customers on a daily basis and can therefore inform marketing of potential changes in purchase patterns. Sales management is usually a separate function and it establishes its own customer goals at the national, regional and local levels. Sales plans set performance targets for each sales representative, and often include share of customer. Finally, share of customer is quite useful when meeting with the company's senior management as it provides insight into specific customers, their value and potential. It assists senior management in understanding how effective and successful their field-based people are in developing their customer relationships.

References

Davis, J. *Magic Numbers for Consumer Marketing,* John Wiley & Sons (Asia) Pte Ltd. 2005: pp. 167–168.

Davis, J. *Measuring Marketing: 103 Key Metrics Every Marketer Needs,* John Wiley & Sons (Asia) Pte Ltd., 2007.

"Market Segmentation/Share of Wallet: Understanding the Characteristics of High-Potential Customers", a case study by Harte-Hanks Research & Analytics.

http://www.hartehanksmi.com/content/pdf/Share%20of%20Wallet%20Case%20Study. pdf

26 Customer-Acquisition Costs[1]

THE DEFINITION

Customer-acquisition costs are those associated with acquiring a new customer.

THE FORMULA AND ITS COMPONENTS

Customer-acquisition costs are calculated by dividing total acquisition expenses by the total number of new customers.

However, there are different opinions as to what constitutes an acquisition expense. For example, rebates and special discounts do not represent an actual cash outlay, yet they have an impact on cash (and, presumably, on the customer). To simplify this process, let's assume your company wants to calculate the cost of acquiring customers through one of its marketing vehicles, CD mailers. AOL used to do this regularly. Parts suppliers and several music distributors use this marketing approach as well, among others.

The formula for customer-acquisition costs in both of the following examples is:

$$C_{ac} = CD_m \times C$$

Where

C_{ac} = customer-acquisition costs
CD_m = number of CD mailers needed to acquire one customer

C = cost to send each mailer

OR

$$C_{ac} = \frac{C}{R_r}$$

Where

R_r = response rate

WHERE'S THE DATA?

Fortunately, there is a sizable body of data from multiple companies and product categories that offer excellent benchmarks for ascertaining direct-marketing metrics. The nature of the target audience determines the kind of data required. Once the target audience has been determined, companies can undertake their own random mailing or can find a list broker who has names for that particular audience. The latter approach is usually more cost-effective, as the ensuing examples will demonstrate.

Also, the costs for the marketing vehicle (in this example, CD mailers, but the same approach can be used with other media) depend on the numbers of CDs sent with each mailing and whether additional literature is included. Response rates are based on industry trends and, therefore, should not be guessed. If the response rates for particular products are not known, these may be obtainable from a reasonably similar industry against which metrics can be benchmarked. In the worst case, if there are no comparable metrics, it is better to assume a conservative response rate that is marginally better for rented lists than a purely random mailing (i.e. 2% response as against 1% response).

A question that inevitably arises is how to determine the number of CD mailers needed to acquire one customer ("CD_m"). This information will vary from one industry to the next and from one country to another. However, the Direct Marketing Association (DMA) website (www.the-dma.org) is a great place to obtain information. Within the site are links to other DMA sites in many countries around the world, including Singapore, Japan, Thailand, Australia and much of Europe, as well as North and South America. Contacting the relevant experts in each location and asking them how and where to find these metrics will help to determine a variety of metrics common to that country. It is important that companies do some homework for the country in which they are interested because often the general metrics cited are U.S.- or Euro-centric and may not be applicable to another specific country or region.

However, once this has been done, the company can then begin to use this formula to analyze its direct-marketing program (CD mailers, in this case). The "magic", then, in this number, is not in the general formula, but in using data and metrics that are consistent with the country context in which you are operating.

CALCULATING IT

Random mailing

Let's assume that the cost of mailing CD mailers is $0.35 each, and the average response rate is 1% (perhaps based on past experience sending mailers, or industry metrics). Thus, one person will respond for every 100 CD mailers sent. The cost of acquiring each customer using a random mailing is:

First formula: $100 \times 0.35 = \$35$
Second formula: $\$0.35 \div 0.01 = \$35$

Depending on the metrics for the particular industry as well as the average order size per customer, $35 to acquire a customer may be perfectly reasonable, too low or too high.

Acquired-list mailing

Smart marketers will not stop there, however. They will want to analyze other options to see if there are more effective ways to acquire customers. They may know, or determine, that renting or acquiring a list of qualified prospects will yield a probable response rate of 3% (three times more effective than a random mailing). This means that for every 100 CD mailers sent, three people will respond. Thus, they may decide to rent a list from a reputable list broker, knowing that the names on the list have a higher likelihood of purchasing the company's products. List brokers are in business to make money and they expend a fair amount of effort to develop their lists through research, so they generally charge a fee. In this example, we'll assume the broker charges $0.25 per name.

The smart marketer can now compare the random mailing to the list mailing and decide which is better.

The cost of acquiring a customer using a list mailing is:

$$\$0.60 \div 0.03 = \$20$$

The $0.60 is the simple result of the cost of mailing each CD, $0.35, plus the cost of acquiring each name, $0.25, and this is then divided by the response rate expected. The upfront cost of sending out CD mailers is clearly more expensive when a list is rented — 71% more in this example. But the overall cost of acquiring customers is reduced substantially *and* the company is reaching an audience more likely to respond favorably to its offer.

WHAT IT MEANS AND POTENTIAL CHALLENGES

Acquisition costs vary across industries and media. When acquisition data is available, it is important that the company determines if it is comparing like with like. As discussed above, using the formula successfully means knowing more about the specific characteristics of the target market. Let's say, for example, that a company's research shows that it will need to send 100 CD mailers to acquire one customer in the target country. It will then have to ask a few simple questions:

- What is the break-even point?

- Do we want to go to this market?

- Is the longer-term market potential large enough to warrant the increased costs?

Reaching this point is not always easy, as customer-acquisition data can be scarce, and the methodology is often foggy. Furthermore, it is a wise move to compare various list brokers and contact a few of their customers to learn just how effective the broker is. While list brokers will generally charge similar rates, there may be variation in quantity and quality of associated information with each name (for example, some lists may come only with name and address, while others may come with name, address, company name, title and so on). Brokers may also charge more for each additional line of information beyond the basic name and address. They usually include several "dummy" contacts in their mailings to ensure that their lists are not used more than once.

Endnote

[1] http://www.marketingterms.com/dictionary/customer_acquisition_cost/

Additional References

There are several online calculators as well as detailed descriptions for determining customer-acquisition cost. Readers are encouraged to visit:
www.positiveresults.com/articles/danger.asp
www.panalysis.com.au/customer_acquisition_cost/
http://multichannelmerchant.com/news/marketing_setting_price_customer/index.html
www.jimnovo.com/LTV.htm
www.clickz.com/experts/crm/analyze_data/article.php/3354331

Break-Even Analysis

THE DEFINITION

Before launching a new product, the management of any company will want to know how many units it must sell at a certain price to break even and offset the costs incurred. Break-even analysis calculates the sales volume at which total costs are equal to total revenues.

THE FORMULAS AND THEIR COMPONENTS

Three break-even analysis methods will be discussed, each addressing different but related parts of a company's needs.

1. Conventional break-even: determining the number of units to be sold where gross revenues equal total costs

2. Break-even market share: translating unit break-even into a market-share equivalent

3. Customer break-even: determining break-even for regular customers as against infrequent customers

WHERE'S THE DATA?

Data for units (forecasts), revenues and costs (price per unit, for example) is found in the accounting and finance departments. Unit costs will either come from suppliers' price summaries or from internal production and operations plans. Unit and revenue forecasts are from each year's budget and business plans and are based on past performance plus any allowance for growth in the coming year that departs (either positively or negatively) from growth rates in prior years.

CALCULATING IT

1. **Conventional break-even** (or break-even volume).[1]

$$BE = \frac{FC}{(P - AVC)}$$

Where

BE   = break-even
FC   = fixed costs
P   = price per unit
AVC = average variable costs

Note that the denominator, $(P - AVC)$, is the contribution margin of each unit sold, known as M_{pu}.

Let's assume an auto-parts company has the following *pro forma* financials for a new product launch:

FC = \$10,000,000

M_{pu} = \$4 (P = \$12, AVC = \$8)

$$BE = \frac{\$10,000,000}{\$4}$$

BE = 2,500,000 units

2. **Break-even market share**[2]

$$BE_{ms} = \frac{BE}{MD} \times 100$$

Where

BE_{ms} = break-even market share
MD   = market demand

If market demand for this product were 50 million units, then the break-even market share would be:

$$BE_{ms} = \frac{2,500,000}{50,000,000} \times 100$$
$$= 5\%$$

3. **Customer break-even**

Assuming that profitable customers are the goal, then it can also be assumed that there are customers who are frequent or regular purchasers of products, and customers who are infrequent or occasional purchasers of products. Both will be discussed here.

Customer break-even analysis is a formula based on a series of data points:

*   Margin on each purchase

*   Survival rate

*   Cost of each marketing communication

*   Expected profit per customer.

Two extended examples will be used to illustrate customer break-even. The second will include margin per unit.

Example 1: An auto-parts company

Let's assume that our auto-parts company launches new products to the market twice per year, in winter and summer. Furthermore, the company's marketing team sends six CD mailers per year in the first year to all customer types. In the second year and beyond, regular customers will continue to receive six CD mailers each year. Less-frequent buyers, though, will receive only two per year thereafter as there is no need for the company to spend the money on them until they start buying more.

Since this company launches new products twice each year, its regular customers receive CD mailers with the same content for three consecutive mailings before changes are made to the mailer. Less-frequent customers receive two different CD mailers with no repetition. The regular customers purchase this company's products three times each year, with an average order size of $30, while the less-frequent buyers purchase once each year, with an average order size of $60.

The retention rate (the rate at which a customer is likely to return the following year) for regular customers is 90%, while the retention rate for less-frequent customers is 45%. Knowing the retention rates helps marketers determine the long-term survival rate of each group of customers (i.e. whether or not they will be around for a given number of years). In the case of the regular customer with a 90% retention rate, his survival factor in year five is 65.6% ($0.90^4 = 0.656$).[3] The less-frequent customer's loyalty or survival rate in year five is 4.1% ($0.45^4 = 0.041$).[4]

The marketer must know the gross margin on each purchase because it helps determine how many purchases a customer type must make over a given period of time before they become profitable. The marketer can then forecast the length of time he will be "investing" in CD mailers before converting a customer to profitability, and senior management of the auto-parts company want to know when their customers acquired through CD mailer marketing will be profitable. The gross margin for these products is 25% of total sales. With these figures, we can construct comparisons between the regular and less-frequent customers with random and purchased list mailings to review the break-even levels.

Random mailing

Regular customer

- Receives six CD mailers per year

- Makes three purchases per year, at $30 per purchase

- There is a 90% retention rate of regular customers who make purchases in the next time period

- Mailing cost = $0.35 per CD mailer

- 1% response rate

- Gross margin = 25%

Acquired-list mailing

Regular customer

- Receives six CD mailers per year

- Makes three purchases per year at $30 per purchase

Figure 27.1   Calculating break-even for regular customers: random mailing

Regular Customers	Year One	Year Two
Margin per Purchase	$7.50 (calculated by multiplying the regular customer's average purchase of $30 by the gross margin of 25%)	$7.50
Retention Rate	100%	90%
CD Mailing Cost	$0.35 × 6 = $2.10	$0.35 x 6 = $2.10
Profit per Customer	3 × 7.50 – 2.10 = $20.40	0.9 x (20.40) = $18.36
Total Profits per Customer (factoring in acquisition costs)	$14.60 (calculated by subtracting customer-acquisition cost — Magic Number 26 — from profit per customer: $20.40–$35 = –$14.60)	$3.76 (calculated as the difference between total profits per customer in Year One and profit per customer in Year Two: $18.36 – $14.60 = $3.76)

- 90% retention rate of regular customers who make purchases in the next time period

- Mailing cost = $0.60 per CD mailer

- 3% response rate

- Gross margin = 25%

Figure 27.2   Calculating break-even for regular customers: acquired mailing

Regular Customers	Year One	Year Two
Margin per Purchase	$7.50	$7.50
Retention Rate	100%	90%
Catalog Mailing Cost	$0.60 x 6 = $3.60	$0.60 x 6 = $3.60
Profit per Customer	3 x 7.50 – 3.60 = $18.90	0.9 x (22.50 – 3.60) = $17.01
Total Profits per Customer (factoring in acquisition costs)	$1.10 (calculated by subtracting customer-acquisition cost — Magic Number 26 — from profit per customer: $18.90 – $20.00 = –$1.10)	$15.91 (calculated as the difference between total profits per customer in Year One and profit per customer in Year Two: $17.01 – $1.10 = $15.91)

In this first set of examples with regular customers it is apparent that acquiring a mailing list enhances profitability over the random mailing. While the cost per mailing is higher by 71%, the customer acquisition cost is lower with the acquired list, making the profit margin higher. In this example, upfront investment in smart marketing (i.e. a mailing list) leads to larger profits. Costs, therefore, are not the only factor that should be considered when choosing a marketing program.

Now we will look at the same framework, but using less-frequent customers.

Random mailing

Less-frequent customer

- Receives six CD mailers per year in the first year, and two per year thereafter

- Makes one purchase per year, at $60 per purchase

- 45% retention rate of regular customers who make purchases in the next time period

- Mailing cost = $0.35 per CD mailer

- 1% response rate

- Gross margin = 25%

Figure 27.3   Calculating break-even for less-frequent customers: random mailing

Less-Frequent Customers	Year One	Year Two	Year Three
Margin	$15	$15	$15
Retention Rate	100%	45%	20.25%
Catalog Mailing Cost	$0.35 x 6 = $2.10	$0.35 x 2 = $0.70	$0.35 x 2 = $0.70
Profit per Customer	$15 – $2.10 = $12.90	0.45 x (15 – 0.70) = $6.44	0.2025 x (15 –0.70) = $2.90
Total Profits per Customer (factoring in acquisition costs)	$(22.10)	($15.66)	($12.76)

It will take several years using this approach before a less-frequent customer becomes profitable. The final example incorporates the cost of an acquired mailing list.

Acquired-list mailing

Less-frequent customer

- Receives six CD mailers per year in year one, and two per year thereafter

- Makes one purchase per year, at $60 per purchase

- There is a 45% retention rate of regular customers who make purchases in the next time period

- Mailing cost = $0.60 per CD mailer

- 3% response rate

- Gross margin = 25%

Figure 27.4   Calculating break-even for less-frequent customers: acquired mailing

Less-Frequent Customers	Year One	Year Two	Year Three
Margin	$15	$15	$15
Retention Rate	100%	45%	20.25%
Catalog Mailing Cost	$0.60 × 6 = $3.60	$0.60 × 2 = $1.20	$0.60 × 2 = $1.20
Profit per Customer	$15 − $3.60 = $11.40	0.45 × (15 − 1.20) = $6.21	0.2025 × (15 − 1.20) = $2.79
Total Profits per Customer (factoring in acquisition costs)	$(8.60)	($2.39)	$.40

Impact on decision making

Customer break-even analysis is straightforward mathematically, but there are several less-visible factors that marketers should consider when calculating it. In these examples, break-even is dependent on list quality, customer-retention rates, gross margin, mailing costs, purchase price and purchase frequency. The analysis ignores other variables such as when a company decides to stop sending its mailers to customers who are no longer active. Determining when to get rid of a customer should be an important part of the planning process, acknowledging that there will be exceptions. Since most business and budget planning is done annually, it is reasonable to use one year as the planning horizon. Therefore, the decision to eliminate customers would occur after the normal sequence of CD mailers has been sent, since it will not be known until the end of a full year that a customer is no longer active. When this occurs, marketers should modify their profit-per-customer calculations by multiplying the previous year's retention rate by the mailing cost. The reason for this is that the previous year is when the customer was last "active", and an influence on the company's profitability.

Marketers may also have other costs that are not reflected in this analysis, such as additional marketing promotions and communications connected to the CD mailer. These should be included in the next mailing analysis. As marketers learn how many products are returned, cancelled or discounted, adjustments to the content and number of mailers will be inevitable.

While customer break-even analysis is a useful tool in assessing the potential of almost any marketing campaign, there are some exceptions. The analysis is less reliable if the marketer is attempting to correlate a general-awareness advertising campaign with increases in customers and sales. Unless the advertising campaign has a specific offer that asks for customers to respond, it is problematic linking an advertising campaign to any specific increase in business.

Example 2: A wallet company

The definitions and formulas are effectively the same, but a different approach to calculating break-even will be described.

In this example, margin per unit (M_{pu}) is included as a variable.

Margin per unit is defined as the amount of money that remains to cover fixed costs after all variable costs are deducted.

Wallets made by this company sell for $10. The retail margin is 30%. The wholesalers who purchase the wallet maker's products take an 8% margin. To determine M_{pu}, information on price, fixed costs and variable costs is needed. The variable costs are $3 per wallet. The total fixed costs (aggregated costs, not per-unit) are $1,800,000 (for salaries, equipment, etc.).

Despite early success, the wallets are facing reduced demand as a result of competition. Furthermore, customers believe the wallets are overpriced. The marketing manager is considering reducing the price by $2. To assist with a strategic response, the marketing manager is considering hiring a consulting firm to provide recommendations and to ensure a high-quality marketing effort. The consulting firm has proposed a contract for $250,000 to help the marketing manager for a month.

The marketing manager is going to make a presentation to the board of directors about her solution for improving the wallet's sales. The plan includes several preliminary formulas needed to determine a defensible break-even level.

The marketing manager knows the following about her products:

- Retail price is $10

- Retail margins are 30%

- Wholesale margins are 8%

- Wallet market is 35 million customers

- Market share is 20%

- Variable costs are $3 per wallet

- Total fixed costs are $1,800,000

- Considering price reduction of $2 per wallet

- Considering hiring a consulting company for $250,000.

She begins by determining the manufacturing sales price (MSP), using the following formula:

$$MSP = P_r - M_r - M_w$$

Where

P_r = retail price
M_r = retail margin percentage
M_w = wholesale margin or mark-up

She calculates MSP as follows:

MSP = $10 − $3 − $0.80 = $6.20

Next, she calculates the margin per unit (M_{pu}):

M_{pu} = MSP − VC

Where

VC = variable costs

This works out to:

M_{pu} = $6.20 − $3 = $3.20

The marketing manager begins the break-even sequence, beginning with break-even volume, using the formula:

$$BE = \frac{FC}{(P - AVC)}$$

Where

FC = Fixed costs

Recall that (P − AVC) is the same as margin per unit (M_{pu}), so the equation simplifies to this:

$$BE = \frac{FC}{M_{pu}}$$

$$BE = \frac{\$1,800,000}{\$3.20}$$

BE = 562,500 wallets

The marketing manager wants to calculate the break-even volume with the $2 price reduction included. She uses the following formula:

$$BE_\Delta = \frac{Original\ M_{pu}}{New\ M_{pu}} \times Original\ BE$$

Where

BE_Δ = break-even volume after price change

Original M_{pu} = $3.20
New M_{pu} = $1.20
Original BE = 562,500 wallets

Solving with the new figures:

$$BE_\Delta = \frac{\$3.20}{\$1.20} \times 562,500$$

$$= 1,500,000 \text{ wallets}$$

Lowering the price by $2 has a significant impact on the break-even figures.

The marketing manager then focuses on determining break-even market share under the regular price, using the formula:

$$BE_{ms} = \frac{BE}{MD} \times 100$$

Where

BE_{ms} = break-even market share

BE = 562,500

MD = market demand

This is calculated as follows:

$$BE_{ms} = \frac{562,500}{35,000,000} \times 100$$

$$= 1.6\%$$

The break-even market share for the price reduction is now calculated:

$$BE_{ms} = \frac{1,500,000}{35,000,000} \times 100$$

$$= 4.3\%$$

Finally, the marketing manager wants to know break-even when it includes the cost of hiring the consulting firm.

$$BE = \frac{FC}{M_{pu}}$$

$$= \frac{\$250,000}{\$3.20}$$

$$= 78,125 \text{ units}$$

Therefore, the marketing manager would need to sell another 78,125 wallets to cover the added cost of the consulting firm.

This alternative analysis shows the different ways to determine break-even. Both approaches in customer break-even highlight the importance of understanding the costs involved in acquiring customers. A good way to use both is to determine the various break-even levels as demonstrated in the second approach, then factor in the marketing costs, customer-retention and customer-response rates to provide an in-depth analysis that provides credible analytical guidance on the measures needed to achieve success.

WHAT IT MEANS AND POTENTIAL CHALLENGES

The different approaches to break-even analysis are important because of the interdependency between measures. For example, break-even analysis influences customer lifetime-value analysis (see Magic Number 29) and it is influenced by customer-acquisition costs.

Knowing the cost of acquiring customers is helpful in determining when a customer will bring profits to the company. Developing long-term customer loyalty is usually the ideal, but only when loyalty leads to ongoing profitability. Companies have to face the decision of keeping or eliminating unprofitable customers. The decision rests on marketing's view of that customer's long-term potential and how long management is willing to wait for the customer to become profitable.

Even with this analysis, actual results will not be 100% consistent with the planning assumptions. But the analysis does provide an added sense of the conditions needed to achieve break-even. It is then the marketing team's responsibility to make it happen. No amount of analysis will make the customer transactions occur.

Historical data will provide most of the information required to perform the break-even calculations. Smart companies know their customers' purchase patterns, whether they sell direct (such as Dell) or they sell through retailers (such as Nike). Start-ups can acquire industry data from benchmark companies in their industry and apply it to their target audience to get a sense of how long it will be before their customers, and ultimately their growing business, are profitable.

Endnotes

[1] Doyle, C. *Collins Internet-Linked Dictionary of Marketing*, Harper Collins, 2003, 2006: p. 47.

[2] Best, R. J. *Market-Based Management: Strategies for Growing Customer Value and Profitability*, Pearson Education, 2005: pp. 255–256.

[3] Loyalty/Survival Factors:
Year $1 = 0.90^0 = 1$
Year $2 = 0.90^1 = 0.9$
Year $3 = 0.90^2 = 0.81$
Year $4 = 0.90^3 = 0.729$
Year $5 = 0.90^4 = 0.656$

[4] Year $1 = 0.45^0 = 1$
Year $2 = 0.45^1 = 0.45$
Year $3 = 0.45^2 = 0.2$
Year $4 = 0.45^3 = 0.091$
Year $5 = 0.45^4 = 0.041$

Additional References

Davis, J. *Magic Numbers for Consumer Marketing*, John Wiley & Sons (Asia) Pte Ltd., 2005: pp. 178–190.

Davis, J. *Measuring Marketing: 103 Key Metrics Every Marketer Needs,* John Wiley & Sons (Asia) Pte Ltd., 2007.

Ofek, E. "Customer Profitability and Lifetime Value", Harvard Business School, #9–503-019, August 7, 2002.

28

Customer Profitability

THE DEFINITION

Customer profitability measures the surplus of revenues over costs at the individual and aggregate customer levels.

THE FORMULA AND ITS COMPONENTS

The formula is:

$$CP = r_t - c_t$$

Where

CP = customer profitability

r_t = revenues from customer during time t

c_t = costs incurred to acquire and support customer during time t

WHERE'S THE DATA?

Customer revenue and costs data is found in the account management summaries maintained by sales management and also in the accounting and/or finance departments.

CALCULATING IT

To illustrate, we will assume that a sales representative's top customer purchased $100,000 in products. The sales person incurred $30,000 in costs to identify, attract and develop the customer relationship (costs included sales promotions, meals, travel and sample products). Therefore, customer profitability was $70,000:

CP = $100,000 − $30,000

= $70,000

WHAT IT MEANS AND POTENTIAL CHALLENGES

Sales and marketing help their companies identify, capture and retain customers. The challenge lies in recognizing, growing and measuring *profitable* customers. For example, a product manufacturer is interested in knowing customer profitability, but not at the individual-consumer level, even though the final end-user is the mass consumer. Acquiring such knowledge would not be an effective use of the sales and marketing effort since the manufacturer is structured to deliver large volumes of product to numerous intermediaries and locations. The sales and marketing effort will instead be directed toward programs that strengthen relationships with wholesalers and retailers. Wholesalers can be offered such incentives as volume pricing, preferred terms and rapid inventory replenishment. Retailers, on the other hand, are targeted with cooperative measures such as slotting allowances, which are fees paid to retailers to ensure product placement on store shelves, and cooperative advertising, which is an agreement between manufacturers and retailers to share product advertising and/or promotion costs. Customer profitability in this situation is an aggregated figure, based on the revenues resulting from sales to wholesalers and the costs associated with those transactions, including any fees paid to retailers.

Customer-profitability models are used by managers to make decisions about allocating resources, particularly the composition of the sales team for individual customers. While all companies have different revenue and cost structures, the simple calculation of revenues minus costs attributable to each customer is sufficient for determining profitability. Sales management must be cognizant that one-time purchases can skew this approach, since it is likely that the costs of acquiring the customer are higher (than those of established customers familiar with the company and its products) relative to the return (measured via increased revenues, profits or both). Therefore, it may be more useful to review loyal customers whose cost to service and purchase patterns are better known.

As shown, the measurement of customer profitability is an exercise in simple calculation. However, astute marketers know that customers have different values. Don Peppers and Martha Rogers, of the Peppers & Rogers Group,[1] are among the leading experts in customer profitability. They assert that not all customers are equal, let alone equally profitable, and their One-to-One model describes approaches for enhancing the value of every customer relationship. Most businesses experience the 80/20 rule (80% of the money comes from 20% of the customers) or a similar dominance of a few customers contributing the majority of the revenues and profits. Determining specific profitability per customer is challenging, however, since costs are hard to assign or allocate accurately. Managers must take the time to understand the profile of customers contributing the most profits and develop programs that continue to develop these important relationships. To find the revenue and cost figures, marketers can begin their research as follows:

Revenues figures

The accounting department in most companies should have sales data attributable to specific products and for specific periods of time. This information is summarized in the income statement, although it is unlikely to have a breakdown of each product's revenue performance. Accounting (or finance) should have a separate transactions record for each product for the period under review, derived from actual payments received from each customer.

Costs figures

Determining costs accurately can be challenging as a consequence of varying materials costs, labor differences, royalties paid to different suppliers, support costs and different marketing programs for each customer. The accounting department will typically aggregate all costs associated with a specific product, allocating it evenly across various customers, even though each customer may have unique purchase patterns.

Endnote

[1] www.peppersandrogers.com

Additional References

Davis, J. *Measuring Marketing: 103 Key Metrics Every Marketer Needs,* John Wiley & Sons (Asia) Pte Ltd., 2007.
Ofek, E. "Customer Profitability and Lifetime Value", Harvard Business School Article, 9-503-019, August 7 (2002).

Customer Equity and Customer Lifetime Value (CLTV)

THE DEFINITION

Conventional wisdom in business tells us that it is more expensive to recruit new customers than to focus on retaining existing customers. Therefore, more management effort should be directed toward developing customer loyalty. Customer-related measures have become a key determinant of marketing effectiveness.

Customer equity is the sum of the present values of the company's future customer cash flows. Customer lifetime value estimates the dollar value (typically, the flow of profits) of a customer's long-term relationship with a company. Together, these two formulas help sales and marketing management measure how much a customer is worth over a specific period of time.

THE FORMULAS AND THEIR COMPONENTS

Two methods are described here, measuring different (but related) factors in CLTV. (There are more-sophisticated treatments for those readers who are interested in exploring this topic further. More information on these is provided in the endnotes.)

Marketing managers developing customer loyalty need to be concerned with maximizing retention and minimizing defection. Retention efforts should involve more than merely maintaining the existing relationship and purchase patterns with existing customers, although that is a good starting point. Given that loyal customers have already "voted" in favor of the company by purchasing its products, the opportunity lies in increasing cross-selling (selling similarly priced complements) and up-selling (selling a more expensive product or complement).[1]

This formula assumes a constant customer-defection rate, a constant net margin and a discount rate.

$$CLTV = \frac{m}{(k + d)}$$

Where

m = constant net margin (profits – retention costs)
k = discount rate
d = constant defection rate

This simplified approach calculates the basic financial value of the customer. Each customer represents potential cross-selling and up-selling value, which is captured by factoring in a constant growth rate, g.

$$CLTV = \frac{m}{(k + d - g)}$$

The growth rate is subtracted because it is unlikely that a customer's long-term growth rate will remain constant. The rate of increasing cross- or up-selling purchases will diminish over time as the customer's added satisfaction and enjoyment from each additional purchase is reduced.

A related approach to CLTV estimates the dollar value (typically, the flow of profits) of a customer's long-term relationship with a company. While it, too, measures how much a customer is worth while remaining a loyal purchaser of a company's products, it also factors in a value for new customers referred by existing customers, adding further value to the relationship developed with the referring customer. As with the first approach, retention is a primary objective. However, this approach does not factor in cross- or up-selling opportunities, focusing instead on new customer referrals. Example two illustrates this method.[2]

The marketing manager needs to be acquainted with the key data associated with the company's loyal customers, derived from:

M = average amount of money spent per purchase
C = average costs to service each purchase
P = number of purchases per year
Y = number of years managers expect to keep this customer
A = new-customer acquisition cost
N = number of new customers referred by original customer
F = customer adjustment factor for the period of time being evaluated.

Allen Weiss, founder and publisher of Marketingprofs.com, describes F, the customer adjustment factor, as follows:

"…(F) captures changes in a customer's behavior over time. If you estimate that the customer will increase the money spent per visit over time (because you estimate you will increase their loyalty), then put in a higher number — say, 1.4. If you estimate the customer will decrease their spending over time, put in a lower number — say, .9 This is obviously a subjective estimate."[3]

Therefore, one is considered steady state, so no correction is needed. The subjective nature of the correction factor reveals the importance of including both qualitative and quantitative measures in the customer analysis. Next, the terms are grouped into individual equations.

$M - C$ = the average gross profit generated by the customer per visit

$P \times Y$ = total number of visits over the customer's lifetime

$A \times N$ = the amount of money saved by the customer's referral

The lifetime value of the customers can now be determined using the formula:

$$CLTV = [(M - C) \times (P \times Y) - A + (A \times N)] \times F$$

Where's the Data?

Retailers can find the average customer-spending information in scanner data simply by adding together total purchases and dividing by the number of customers (or transactions), depending on how sophisticated the retailer's point-of-purchase system is. Non-retail businesses capture customer data through the field-sales force and its call reports, as well as account management profiles which are maintained by customer account teams. Average costs are found in the income statement or daily bookkeeping records. The forecast numbers are estimates, based either on historical experience, industry benchmarks or perhaps even new services, products or technologies that management believe influence customers' buying patterns. Finding out accurately the number of new customers an existing customer refers to your company requires a fair amount of knowledge of each individual customer and a basic database designed to track these kinds of activities. The correction factor is an estimate based on management judgment born of experience. If sales management know their business or have a sense of how competitors perform, then they should be able to estimate a reasonable correction factor.

CALCULATING IT

To illustrate, let's assume the management of a hotel chain wishes to determine the lifetime value of an average customer. Management review the guest statistics for their hotels:

M = average amount of money spent per purchase (guest) = $220
C = average costs to service each purchase (guest) = $70
P = number of purchases/visits per year = 3
Y = number of years managers expect to keep this customer = 20
A = new-customer acquisition cost = $25
N = number of new customers referred by original customer = 5
F = customer-adjustment factor = 1.3

CLTV of the average guest equals $11,830, as shown below:

$$\{(\$220 - \$70) \times (3 \times 20) - \$25 + (25 \times 5)\} \times 1.3 = \$11,830$$

In this illustration, hotel management have determined that their loyal customers are likely to spend more in the future with each visit; hence the higher customer-adjustment factor.

WHAT IT MEANS AND POTENTIAL CHALLENGES

CLTV in these approaches can be influenced by what data is used and how it is interpreted. For example, determining the average spending per customer is dependent on whether sales representatives are using the number of transactions or of customers in their calculation. If a manager adds together total purchases and divides by the number of transactions, then the value of some customers may be under-represented since their separate multiple purchases would be viewed purely as if they were separate customers. On the other hand, accurately determining actual customer purchases requires a more sophisticated tool, which not all sellers may have. In the case of retail businesses, loyalty cards that can be scanned with each purchase are an example. However, loyalty cards may not be used consistently by customers, which can skew the analysis.

Cost figures are quite challenging to determine at the individual-purchase level. Are managers measuring the cost of the entire operation at the time the customer made his or her purchase? Or are they assessing the costs specific to that transaction? If managers are measuring the costs specific to the transaction, they will find them very hard to determine with any degree of precision. Therefore, it is most useful if managers determine a set of costs that are normal for each operation and that are applicable to customer-specific transactions, then apply these consistently every time costs are measured.

There is no single formula that is perfect and the same is true with CLTV. Even with more-sophisticated modeling, managers must be comfortable knowing that their customers simply will not behave according to predictions. This is similar to the economic theory that assumes a rational customer. It is convenient from a modeling and analytical point of view, but it does not reflect the nuances of day-to-day consumer behavior.

The important takeaway for sales and marketing managers is the sizable long-term value represented by a loyal customer, which should provide the incentive to develop marketing programs designed to reinforce retention. The process reinforces why businesses should try to develop long-term relationships rather than short-term or, worse, one-time purchase gains.

Endnotes

[1] Reibstein, D. and R. Srivastava. "Metrics for Linking Marketing to Financial Performance". Working paper submitted to Marketing Science Institute, October 19, 2004: pp. 8–9.

[2] Adapted from http://www.marketingprofs.com/5/weiss7.asp

[3] http://www.marktingprofs.com/5/weiss7.asp

Additional References

Lennon, K. N., R. T. Rust and V. A. Zeithaml. "Customer-Centered Brand Management", *Harvard Business Review,* September 2004.

Additional resources about customer lifetime value for the enthusiastic and the curious:

http://www-stat.stanford.edu/~saharon/papers/lty.pdf

http://hbswk.hbs.edu/item.jhtml?id=1436&t=marketing

http://executive.education.wharfon.upenn.edu/globals/documents/metrics.pdf

http://www.interactionmetrics.com/custormer_equity.htm

30 Churn Rate and Customer Loss

THE DEFINITION

Churn is a measure of customer attrition, measuring the percentage of customers a company loses over a given period of time. Customer loss measures, as the name implies, the actual number of customers lost.

When a company attracts a customer, the next step is to acquire and retain that customer. Not all customers are loyal or profitable or desirable. Some cost more to service than others, for example. Nevertheless, a vital component of a successful customer strategy is converting first-time buyers into long-term, profitable relationships. Of the customers initially attracted, some inevitably choose to move on to another company and its products.

THE FORMULA AND ITS COMPONENTS

Calculating churn results in the percentage of its customers a business loses over a specific period of time. The formula is as follows:

$$\text{Churn} = \frac{C_t}{C_{at}} \times 100$$

Where

C_t = the number of customers a business loses over time period t
C_{at} = the number of active customers at the start of time period t

Calculating customer loss is a simple subtraction, as follows:

$$\text{Customer Loss} = C_{bt} - C_{et}$$

Where

C_{bt} = the number of active customers at beginning of time period t

C_{et} = the number of active customers at end of time period t

WHERE'S THE DATA?

Sales, customer-support, customer-service, telemarketing and even customer-account managers in accounting track data on customer accounts, including total accounts, active and inactive, new accounts and cancelled or departed accounts. Churn figures typically come from one of two sources in these departments: reactive, or post-customer-departure, reports; and proactive, or pre-customer-departure, reports.

Reactive reports are generated by any of several key areas in a company, depending on its size, complexity and customer-account practices. As the name implies, reactive reports capture customer departures after customers have contacted the company and indicated they are leaving. It is a more straightforward metric, although it can also be frustrating since it is usually much harder to convince an already-lost customer to return. Proactive efforts attempt to *predict* which customers are likely to leave, allowing sales representatives the opportunity to target them with new programs and incentives designed to retain them and, thereby, reduce churn.[1]

CALCULATING IT

For churn, let's assume a sales territory within a large company had 100 customers at the start of the year and 23 customer losses during the year. Churn is 23%:

$$\text{Churn} = \frac{23}{100} \times 100$$
$$= 23\%$$

It is quite simple calculating customer loss, except that we are now comparing customers at the start and end of the specific time period, with the difference being the customer-loss figure. Assuming the company started the year with 100 customers and ended the year with 77, then the actual number of customers lost is 23:

Customer loss = 100 − 77
               = 23

WHAT IT MEANS AND POTENTIAL CHALLENGES

Losing customers is expensive since money and resources have been invested to educate and attract them. Once customers have "voted" in favor of a company's products (by purchasing them), sales management's next step is to leverage the initial purchase into a profitable long-term relationship. For planning and budgeting purposes, sales management need to see how many customers have been lost and how many retained, so that future plans, goals and quotas can be adjusted to reduce losses.

Churn is commonly used in the telecommunications industry, particularly in the United States (where consumers regularly receive marketing communications in the form of discounts, low- or no-penalty provider-switching plans, and a wide variety of pricing schemes within), but increasingly too around the world as telecommunications is deregulated. It is a highly competitive, commodity-driven market in which providers' offerings are often indistinguishable from one another. Consequently, consumers frequently switch service providers to pay the lowest possible price. The average churn varies within the telecommunications industry. In the wireless sector, annual churn rates have ranged from 23.4% to 46%.[2] The Internet sector confronts similarly high churn rates, ranging from 21% to 63%.[3]

It is important that sales management learn why customers have left so they can reduce churn in the future through enhanced selling practices, revised marketing-communications programs, improved product offerings, better pricing and more effective targeting of customers. Most businesses regularly confront churn challenges, trying to develop strategies and programs that will minimize it since losing a customer is often expensive in time (amount of time invested to attract and retain a customer), resources (manpower deployed to service customers) and money (the actual outlay of cash spent on customer-development programs). Churn rates also have an impact on CLTV analysis (see Magic Number 29) since a higher churn rate indicates customers are not staying long with the company, an outcome that leads to higher costs since more money has to be invested to educate and attract new customers.

Churn is somewhat similar to retention (described as "the percentage of a company's customers that it is able to retain over a specified time period"[4]), but there are subtle differences. Churn is calculated with former/lost customers *only,* while retention can be determined with former *or* existing customers.[5] Churn research focuses on why customers left, whereas retention focuses on how to maintain and increase loyalty. Furthermore, churn is subject to slight interpretation, blurring the distinction even more. In our telecommunications example, different providers may use slightly different methodologies in calculating churn. In the United States, when a customer moves from one area to another, and consequently changes telephone numbers, yet remains with the same provider, the provider might count this move as churn. Alternatively, when a customer's service contract expires and that same customer selects a different plan with the same provider, this may also be counted as churn. In these two instances, the customer has remained with the provider, but individual circumstances have created the need to change the previous plan.

Sales and marketing management must be clear on their definition of churn since it affects the kinds of sales and marketing programs designed to attract and retain customers in the future. A conservative definition of churn suggests that it pertains only to customers the company has lost to a competitor, as opposed to those who have simply moved to another division or product within the same firm. This definition would lead the curious marketer to explore why the customer switched to a competitor, whether this is an isolated move or an indication of a larger, unsettling trend and, consequently, how to improve the situation for remaining and new customers. However, large companies (such as those in the telecommunications industry) often "lose" customers to another division. Corporate marketers, with broad strategic responsibilities for marketing across the entire company, may view this as retention since the customer remains with the company overall. But sales representatives, divisional and/or product-line marketers may count this as churn and, therefore, will focus on measures to reduce it in the future.

Whether a customer is lost to a direct competitor or to another division within the same company, sales management can use this as an opportunity to improve their selling techniques, including customer presentations, customer analysis, proposal development, and closing sales.

Similar to churn, customer loss is an effective tool for assessing the continued value of an existing product to customers as it matures over time. If an existing product is losing customers or revenues, sales management is faced with three choices: invest in new strategies and tactics to improve acceptance of the product and increase the product's profitability as well; stop doing business with unprofitable or low-margin customers; or remove the product from the product portfolio.

The logic of the formula assumes that C_{bt} is larger than C_{et}, resulting in a number equal to or greater than zero. The reason is simple: if C_{et} were larger than C_{bt}, then it would suggest a gain in total customers over the same period of time. Assuming customer losses are larger than customer gains during the time period being measured, sales representatives can begin analyzing the defections to determine if there are any patterns and their potential causes. If the losses occur in only one period and not over several periods, then it may be an anomalous event requiring only minor analysis to ensure the causes are limited. However, if customer losses persist, it may well signal significant problems, including one or more of the following:

- A decline in the level of trust customers have in the company's products

- Products that are no longer relevant to the customer's needs

- A decrease in quality

- The price-value relationship is no longer attractive

- Competitors' offerings are better/cheaper/more trustworthy/more innovative

- A shift or changing trend in the overall consumer market

- A dysfunctional relationship with the customer.

While sales people do not like to lose customers, it is important to measure the losses and understand the causes in order to eliminate or at least minimize them in the future. A persistent pattern of customer losses will inevitably have a negative impact on cash flow unless those customers that remain are extraordinarily profitable (which would suggest the customers lost are acceptable to the company since they were generating losses). Determining the actual causes of customer loss is, of course, easier said than done since the influencing factors can be numerous and quite complex. The potential complexity should not deter sales management from undertaking the analysis, however, since the resulting benefits will include a clearer understanding of the variables that influenced the loss.

Sales management should create a plan for retaining high-profit customers and enhancing their value to the company. However, this can be a difficult analysis to get right, since high-value customers often have complicated relationships with companies across multiple business areas, from products and services to support and finance. Customers may switch from one product line to another, but within the same company. Some managers may consider this as customer loss for one product, while others may see this as a gain for the company, albeit in a different area.

The U.S. auto industry used customer-satisfaction scores for years, assuming, incorrectly, that it was a predictor of happiness with the product and, indirectly, an indicator of product and even financial success. Yet through the mid 1990s, while the customer-satisfaction scores remained high, the repurchase rate stayed between 30% and 40%, suggesting a customer loss of 60% to 70%. Interestingly, it is easy to imagine the bottom-line impact if the auto industry could reduce customer losses to "only" 50% or 55%.[6]

Endnotes

[1] Neslin, Scott A., Dartmouth College; Gupta, Sunil, Columbia University; Kamakura, Wagner, Duke University; Lu, Junxiang, Comerica Bank; Mason, Charlotte, University of North Caroline: *Defection Detection: Improving Predictive Accuracy of Customer Churn Models:* pp. 4–7, March 2004.

[2] Ibid p. 3

[3] Ibid

[4] Davis, J. *Measuring Marketing: 103 Key Metrics Every Marketer Needs,* John Wiley & Sons (Asia) Pte Ltd., 2007: Chapter 28.

[5] Reichheld, F. F. "Learning from Customer Defections", *Harvard Business Review,* March-April, 1996: pp. 4–5.

[6] http://www.polarismr.com/customer_ret.htm

Additional Reference

http://www.investopedia.com/terms/c/churnrate.asp

31

Customer Franchise

THE DEFINITION

This metric identifies those customers who are regular, core buyers. Since marketing is responsible for creating and developing the customer base, marketers need to evaluate which customers have the highest value. This will allow them to determine how best to deploy marketing resources. Sales management's role is to deploy the most talented sales professionals in a way that maximizes the financial return on committed buyers, both by converting uncommitted, high-potential buyers to customers and developing committed customers further.

THE FORMULA AND ITS COMPONENTS[1]

Committed buyers have the highest likelihood of continuing to purchase the company's products. Additionally, sales revenues include purchases from less-committed buyers. The following formula represents a company's total sales derived from a combination of committed and uncommitted buyers:

$$\text{Sales} = (P_1 \times N_1) + (P_2 \times N_2)$$

Where

P_1 = probability of customer buying if committed
N_1 = number of committed buyers
P_2 = probability of customer buying if uncommitted
N_2 = number of uncommitted buyers

WHERE'S THE DATA?

The sales department's customer reports from each sales representative will have data on committed and uncommitted buyers. Committed buyers are known, since they are existing customers. Uncommitted buyers are high-potential prospective customers in each sales representative's "pipeline" or list of existing and high-potential customers.

CALCULATING IT

Let's assume that a hypothetical firm, Machined Industrial Parts (MIP), has 1,000 committed customers (industrial manufacturers with machinery using MIP's parts) who believe in MIP's products. Of these, 60% buy products each year. MIP also has another 1,000 uncommitted customers who have purchased their products infrequently or just once. They also buy the products of MIP's competitors. Since these uncommitted customers purchase non-MIP products as well, their probability of purchasing solely from MIP is, the company estimates, 20%.

$$\text{Sales} = (60\% \times 1{,}000) + (20\% \times 1{,}000)$$
$$= 600 + 200$$
$$= 800$$

Sales management might be tempted to increase the sales from the committed and uncommitted buyers, spending money and time trying to convert the uncommitted buyers into higher-probability committed buyers. Let's assume sales management pursue this and convert 50 buyers:

$$\text{Sales} = (60\% \times 1{,}050) + (20\% \times 950)$$
$$= 630 + 190$$
$$= 820$$

This represents an improvement. However, if sales management chooses to try to convert uncommitted buyers, it is reasonable to assume that a disproportionate share of the sales department budget will be spent on educating these uncommitted buyers, requiring that sales reps spend more time with these customers. The certainty of conversion is unknown, but it is safe to assume that only some of the uncommitted buyers will convert and, of these, not all will become *high-probability* committed buyers.

Common sense suggests that sales management should focus their efforts on the customer franchise, since committed buyers have a higher probability of buying in the first place and have demonstrated their loyalty and commitment already. Let's now assume that sales management are able to increase the probability of purchase from the committed buyers to 65%, with the uncommitted-buyer efforts remaining the same:

$$\text{Sales} = (65\% \times 1{,}000) + (20\% \times 1{,}000)$$
$$= 650 + 200$$
$$= 850$$

Another option would be to increase the number of committed buyers. The company's marketing research may have revealed that there is a segment of customers whose characteristics are similar to those of its committed buyers, so sales management allocate a portion of the sales department budget specifically to these new customers and attracts 50 more as a result:

$$\text{Sales} = (60\% \times 1{,}050) + (20\% \times 1{,}000)$$
$$= 630 + 200$$
$$= 830$$

50 new committed buyers have been attracted, with the overall sales result still better than the first option above of allocating sales resources toward converting uncommitted buyers.

WHAT IT MEANS AND POTENTIAL CHALLENGES

Assuming sales management have concluded that uncommitted buyers are not to be the focus of their selling efforts, then there are three ways to improve sales: increase the probability of buying from committed buyers; increase the number of committed buyers; or a combination of both.

To increase the probability of buying from committed buyers, promotions may be most effective approach. Field-sales representatives may know that a given buyer will purchase at least 60% of the time, so the challenge is to increase this by increasing usage. Promotions are an effective method for doing so. However, the disadvantage is that the promotion may only "spike" usage for the duration of the promotion without effecting a permanent increase in the probability of purchase. To sustain the desired levels of higher probability of purchase, sales representatives will have to engage in more-sophisticated sales and relationship-building techniques that offer higher value without resorting to discount-driven promotions. Otherwise, the committed buyers will become trained to expect discounts and may wait to purchase when the next discount is offered. This unfortunate result has the effect of increasing the probability of purchase but, over the longer-term, actually reducing profitability.

To increase the number of committed buyers, sales management can ask marketing to focus more on advertising, and on product-and-service enhancements and similar value-added activities. This approach has the distinct advantage of attracting more committed buyers and eliminates the influence of discounts. This is arguably a more responsible long-term approach since it yields more committed buyers who, when purchasing, pay full price. Sales management's job is effectively easier since the product they represent is now a better competitive offering, overcoming potential customer objections.

The final option, improving the probability of purchase *and* increasing the number of committed buyers may sound appealing (after all, who wouldn't want a larger pool of committed buyers who have a high probability of purchase as well?), but sales and marketing management must be aware of the challenges. First, the sales and marketing expense is likely to be higher since both departments are allocating dollars both to increase the purchase probability through developing promotions and increase committed buyers through increased advertising activities. Second, the same risk exists when sales management tries to increase the probability of purchase through promotions: long-term margins may suffer. In effect, the company may actually end up with a larger pool of committed buyers, all of whom now expect discounts, making the cost of servicing each customer higher than before.

The bottom-line lesson is that the customer franchise is a valuable measure to help sales and marketing management understand how to use the levers at their disposal to increase sales profitability and effectiveness for the business.

Endnote

[1] Wilson, Richard M. S. and C. Gilligan. *Strategic Marketing Management: Planning, Implementation & Control* © 2005 p. 527.

Additional Reference

Davis, J. *Measuring Marketing: 103 Key Metrics Every Marketer Needs*, John Wiley & Sons (Asia) Pte Ltd., 2007.

New-Customer Gain

THE DEFINITION

New-customer gain is defined as the number of new customers acquired by a given company over a specific period of time, expressed as a percentage. The calculation helps sales management measure the success of their efforts in this regard.

THE FORMULA AND ITS COMPONENTS

The formula for calculating this is:

$$NCG = C_{et} - C_{bt}$$

Where

NCG = new-customer gain
C_{et} = the number of customers at end of time period t
C_{bt} = the number of customers at beginning of time period t

Alternatively, new-customer gain can be measured as:

$$NCG = \frac{C_n}{C_{bt}} \times 100$$

Where

NCG = new customer gain
C_n = the number of new customers acquired during time period t
C_{bt} = the number of customers at beginning of time period t

WHERE'S THE DATA?

See Magic Number 30 on churn.

CALCULATING IT

Let's assume a sales territory within a large company has 120 customers at the end of the year and had 100 customers at the start.

NCG = 120 − 100 = 20 (or 20%)

Using the alternative formula, we arrive at the same answer:

$$NCG = \frac{20}{100} \times 100$$
$$= 20\%$$

On a general business level, professional sport provides an interesting example on new-customer gain. Most of the professional leagues around the world have programs designed to attract new fans. The National Football League (NFL) is the governing body for professional football in the United States. The NFL has 32 teams, and each team develops its team and market appeal based on the needs of the city in which it is located. Most teams have a variety of mechanisms to attract new fans, including different pricing programs. These programs include:

- Single-game tickets (purchased for specific games, often on the game-day itself)

- Season tickets (tickets for every home game paid-in-full prior to the commencement of the season)

- Personal seat licenses (PSLs — a one-time purchase of a specific seat and its associated rights). PSLs theoretically allow a fan to own a specific seat forever. Clubs charge the fan for the annual season tickets but the PSL guarantees that the fan will have the same seat every year. The same applies, too, for luxury boxes/suites that accommodate several people and include more spacious and comfortable seats and other amenities such as televisions and personalized food service. The objective of an NFL sports franchise (like any business, for that matter) is to maximize revenues and attract as many new customers as possible.

WHAT IT MEANS AND POTENTIAL CHALLENGES

New-customer gain provides a basic gauge of a new product's acceptance in the market or of its success in attracting a new segment to the company's products. As with most sales-management measures, this calculation requires sales management to investigate the sources of the gain to better understand how to capture additional gains in the future. Sales management should work with their marketing counterparts to identify the factors that contributed to the gain in new customers. Did the gains result from new marketing, new sales techniques, or both? If so, which programs and techniques yielded the greatest return? It is important to compare the actual costs of acquiring each new customer to the additional revenues and profits generated. While start-up companies and new product launches regularly incur higher costs than revenues until they have developed their customer base and resulting revenue stream, it would be disadvantageous to spend more on acquiring new customers than the business gains in new revenues for a sustained period of time.

Often, organizations may encounter difficulty in determining new-customer gain as a number of other factors are involved. For example, customers may switch from one line of product to another, but within the same company. While some companies may consider this as customer gain for one product, others may ignore such movements. However, sales management must be clear in explaining what they are measuring. For example, Steve Jobs of Apple Computer announced at the January 2006 MacWorld Conference that in the first quarter of fiscal 2006, the company sold 14 million iPods compared to 4.5 million iPods in the same quarter of 2005.[1] By most standards, this represents a significant increase in units sold. Does the year-over-year increase mean that Apple acquired 9.5 million new customers as well? That is unlikely. Undoubtedly, some customers bought more than one iPod. It is reasonable to assume, however, that some of the 9.5 million increase included several million more customers. It is tempting to misread or misjudge what this metric is describing, so sales management must understand and communicate clearly what the result of the calculation means.

Endnote

[1] CNN.com, January 11, 2006. http://edition.cnn.com/2006/TECH/ptech/01/10/apple.macworld.reut/index.html

Additional Reference

Davis, J. *Measuring Marketing: 103 Key Metrics Every Marketer Needs,* John Wiley & Sons (Asia) Pte Ltd., 2007.

Return On Customer^{sm}

THE DEFINITION

According to Don Peppers and Martha Rogers of Peppers and Rogers Group, a leading consultancy focused on improving business performance through a customer-centric focus, Return on Customer^{sm} (ROC^{sm}) is another way of measuring shareholder value. One benefit of using ROC^{sm} is that calculating it can help sales people more clearly understand how to tailor their offering to various customers to create value faster. Marketers are familiar with the targeting and segmentation techniques designed to help them understand their customers, including:

- Geographic

- Demographic

- Psychographic

- Product uses

- Segmentation options ranging from a single-segment emphasis to full market coverage.

A sizable investment in time, money and resources is usually necessary to gather enough useful details about customers to ensure that the ensuing marketing programs (advertising, pricing, promotions) are properly designed and directed to the most appropriate audience.

Similarly, sales management invests significant time, resources and energy in converting prospective customers targeted by marketing into committed customers. This investment includes educating sales representatives about the new customer segments and training that updates and teaches selling techniques. Both sales and marketing management must evaluate the potential return on these customer investments. Calculating Return on Customer[sm] enables sales and marketing to more confidently demonstrate that their customer investments are paying off.

THE FORMULA AND ITS COMPONENTS[1]

Return on Customer[sm] is represented by the following formula:

$$ROC^{sm} = \frac{\pi_i + \Delta CE_i}{CE_i - 1}$$

Where

ROC^{sm} = return on customer

π_i = cash flow from customers during period i

ΔCE_i = change in customer equity during period i

CE_{i-1} = customer equity at beginning of period i

WHERE'S THE DATA?

The customer data for these analyses is in the detailed customer development plans and budgets developed by sales and marketing. These plans provide explicit guidance on the uses of each department's budgeted funds for customer development. The actual end-of-period numbers used for review are summarized by the finance or accounting departments for the company's financial statements.

CALCULATING IT

Peppers and Rogers illustrate Return on Customer[sm] with two useful charts. The first one illustrates a steady customer response rate over time to sales and marketing programs.

The second example assumes a declining response rate over time. A number of factors can contribute to a decreasing response rate, including customers' weariness from repeated messages or uninspiring offers. As Peppers and Rogers argue, companies risk destroying customer equity, even as they appear to be making a profit.

	Year 1	Year 2	Year 3	Year 4
Total prospects	1,000,000	1,000,000	1,000,000	1,000,000
Response rate	1%	1%	1%	1%
Cost per campaign	$1,000,000	$1,000,000	$1,000,000	$1,000,000
Cash flow per campaign	$1,250,000	$1,250,000	$1,250,000	$1,250,000
Profit per campaign	$250,000	$250,000	$250,000	$250,000
Profit per year (6 campaigns)	$1,500,000	$1,500,000	$1,500,000	$1,500,000
Year-end customer equity	$6,000,000	$6,000,000	$6,000,000	$6,000,000
Change in customer equity	—	—	—	—
Total value created	$1,500,000	$1,500,000	$1,500,000	$1,500,000
Return on customer	—	25%	25%	25%

	Year 1	Year 2	Year 3	Year 4
Total prospects	1,000,000	1,000,000	1,000,000	1,000,000
Response rate	1%	0.95%	0.90%	0.85%
Cost per campaign	$1,000,000	$1,000,000	$1,000,000	$1,000,000
Cash flow per campaign	$1,250,000	$1,187,500	$1,125,000	$1062,500
Profit per campaign	$250,000	$187,500	$125,000	$62,500
Profit per year (6 campaigns)	$1,500,000	$1,125,000	$750,000	$375,000
Year-end customer equity	$6,000,000	$4,500,000	$3,000,000	$1,500,000
Change in customer equity	—	$(1,500,000)	$(1,500,000)	$(1,500,000)
Total value created	$1,500,000	$(375,000)	$(750,000)	$(1,125,000)
Return on customer	—	(6.3%)	(16.7%)	(37.5%)

WHAT IT MEANS AND POTENTIAL CHALLENGES

The objectives of sales and marketing programs designed to grow customer business must be clearly explained from multiple perspectives. Depending on the business need, a marketer may be tempted to boost short term revenues using promotional offers and sales representatives may want to offer a discount to encourage an uncertain customer to purchase. These efforts may improve sales (and perhaps profits), but the cost may be the loss of loyal customers, the destruction of customer equity, or both. Therefore, sales and marketing managers have to assess the implications of their customer plans before launching them. Both sales and marketing are responsible for measuring the effectiveness of the customer programs. The implications of declining customer equity must be recognized by sales and marketing people when they are designing their programs. A promotional campaign with an attractive price offer may increase sales, but it may also dilute any brand premium that had been previously built over time.

References

Peppers, D. and M. Rogers *Return on Customer: Creating Maximum Value From Your Scarcest Resource*, 2005, Don Peppers and Martha Rogers, Published by Doubleday, a division of Random House, Inc. Chapter 1 "An Open Letter to Wall Street" pp. 16–18.

Davis, J. *Measuring Marketing: 103 Key Metrics Every Marketer Needs*, John Wiley & Sons (Asia) Pte Ltd., 2007

Note

[1] Return on Customer and ROC are registered service marks of Peppers and Rogers Group, a division of Carlson Marketing Group, Inc. Readers who are interested in a more comprehensive treatment of ROC^{sm} are encouraged to review Peppers and Rogers' book as footnoted above. Furthermore, their website, www.peppersandrogers. com, provides additional insight into their consulting and research work.

34 Program/Non-Program Ratio

THE DEFINITION

The program/non-program ratio compares the amount of money spent on selling activities designed to create value to the amount spent on the overhead and administrative inputs needed to support those activities. The result is a measure of selling efficiency, with higher ratios indicating a more efficient sales effort.

THE FORMULA AND ITS COMPONENTS[1]

The formula here is:

$$PNPR = \frac{P_t}{TP_t}$$

Where

PNPR = program/non-program ratio
P_t = amount spent (\$) on selling program in time period t
TP_t = total support (\$) spent in time period t

Note: Total support comprises program and non-program expenses.

WHERE'S THE DATA?

The data for both sales-program spending and support spending is found in the sales department and customer-support budgets. The same information will also be found in the company's accounting statements.

CALCULATING IT

Rhodesian Ridgeback Rescue, Inc.(RRRI),[2] a not-for-profit organization in North America dedicated to finding homes and basic medical care for orphaned Rhodesian Ridgeback dogs, reported that its 2004 program expenses were $93,537 and its non-program expenses were $18,616, for a total expense of $112,153. RRRI's non-program activities are related to the administrative costs associated with fundraising and other administrative expenses, including telephone, legal and postage. Its PNPR is thus calculated as follows:

$$PNPR = \frac{\$93,537}{\$112,153} \times 100\%$$

$$= 83\%$$

WHAT IT MEANS AND POTENTIAL CHALLENGES

There is little question that the sales department's purpose is to increase revenues, profits, and the total number and quality of customers. This is an important role, and a vital source of success for companies. Given this mandate, companies must ask how efficient their sales efforts are in relation to the amount of money invested in this area.

PNPR is a general guideline for measuring sales efficiency and is one of several steps sales management would undertake to evaluate the effectiveness of the company's selling program. Since a higher ratio is desirable, they would use the result to set goals for the next budget period, proposing programs for improving the ratio by increasing the percentage. The challenge lies in determining the actual variables that comprise program and non-program activities, so sales management will need to recommend a clear set of definitions that are agreed upon with senior management. This will ensure that the metric measures the same variables each time. For example, a sales manager may define program activities as any programs that boost the sales of a specific product. This would include promotions, specific advertising, price lists and discount programs. Correspondingly, non-program activities might include legal and accounting costs, plus an allocation of payroll for administrative tasks unrelated to the programs.

Endnotes

[1] LaPointe, P. *Marketing by the Dashboard Light,* Patrick LaPointe, 2005: p. 99.
[2] http://www.ridgebackrescue.org/articles/2005_may_year_2004_in_review.pdf

Additional Reference

Davis, J. *Measuring Marketing: 103 Key Metrics Every Marketer Needs,* John Wiley & Sons (Asia) Pte Ltd., 2007.

35

Program/Payroll Ratio

THE DEFINITION

The program/payroll ratio compares the amount of money spent on sales activities designed to create value to the amount spent on payroll in support of those activities. Magic Number 34 described the program/non-program ratio, which compares costs devoted to value-producing sales management activities with support inputs such as overhead, administration and legal costs. Sales management can gain further insight by focusing specifically on the ratio of program expenses to payroll, removing other overhead and administrative costs.

THE FORMULA AND ITS COMPONENTS

The formula for this metric is as follows:

$$PPR = \frac{P_t}{MP_t}$$

Where

PPR = program/payroll ratio

P_t = sales-program spending ($) in time period t

MP_t = sales payroll ($) in time period t

Note: Sales payroll spending covers salary, benefits and related payroll costs.

WHERE'S THE DATA?

The data for both sales-program spending and sales payroll is found in the sales department budgets.

CALCULATING IT

If a company had $1 million in total selling expense, of which $400,000 was program spending and $600,000 was payroll, then the PPR would be:

$$PPR = \frac{\$400,000}{\$600,000} \times 100\%$$

$$= 67\%$$

As selling-program expenditures are increased (assuming payroll remains constant), the percentage increases, and as program expenditures are decreased, the percentage decreases as well. The ratio is useful primarily as a period-to-period comparison for the same company, since competitor and industry comparisons offer little meaningful guidance as a result of differences in budget priorities.

WHAT IT MEANS AND POTENTIAL CHALLENGES

Each company has different guidelines for payroll and non-payroll activities. A worst-case scenario would have little or no program expenses, meaning most expenses would be for payroll activities. Organizations with this imbalance are not likely to last long, since salaries are being paid to managers who are providing little or no customer-related development activities. Ratios are subject to interpretation or even abuse by those seeking to disguise or re-allocate expenses to create a more favorable PPR result. To improve efficiency legitimately, sales management would need to argue persuasively for an increase in the amount of program-related spending (discount programs, promotions, entertainment expense to develop customer relationships) while holding payroll expenses constant (or not increasing them as much as program expenditures). Since the goal is sales efficiency, sales management have a fiduciary and ethical responsibility to portray their budget requests accurately. Patrick LaPointe, Managing Partner of Marketing NPV,[1] points out that industrial and B2B firms often have high payroll costs relative to their advertising expenditures, which suggests that the organizations are spending a great deal of money on non-customer-facing activities. B2B organizations usually have higher sales and business-development costs as well, since a significant portion of their customer activities are related to one-to-one selling and relationship development. The key is for each firm to understand its own goals and establish agreed definitions of program and non-program activities.

Endnote

[1] LaPointe, P. *Marketing by the Dashboard Light,* Patrick LaPointe, 2005: p. 99.

Additional Reference

Davis, J. *Measuring Marketing: 103 Key Metrics Every Marketer Needs,* John Wiley & Sons (Asia) Pte Ltd., 2007.

36 Time–Driven Activity– Based Costing

THE DEFINITION

Time-driven activity-based costing (TDABC) is designed to help company management measure the indirect costs involved in supporting their customers.

Sales management must measure customer profitability effectively, accounting for the work inputs that support customer-related activities. Robert S. Kaplan, a professor at Harvard Business School, has pioneered much of the research about activity-based costing (ABC). Kaplan suggests that some companies have struggled to measure costs successfully using ABC because of implementation challenges (including development costs) and the challenge of complexity within their own operations, which were not always adequately captured by ABC. His solution is time-driven activity-based costing (TDABC).

THE FORMULA AND ITS COMPONENTS[1]

TDABC measures two factors: the cost per hour of each department working on customer-, product- or service-related activities; and the specific time devoted to the activities themselves. The formula is as follows:

$$TC = C_h \times T_u$$

Where

TC = total cost
C_h = cost per hour
T_u = time in units

WHERE'S THE DATA

Data for cost per hour will be kept in the company's financial statements, human resources departments, and customer-support departments. With today's sophisticated software technology, engineering and other customer-support operations can be tracked to the minute. The astute sales professional is encouraged to review these costs periodically to maintain his or her understanding of current costs, thereby helping support the final pricing proposals they make to customers.

Data for time in units (per support call) is also found in the tracking software, usually in productivity reports. Reviewing this information will provide the total time spent on customers, the total number of customers and the average time spent per customer.

CALCULATING IT

Database companies sell business software. The software is usually part of a packaged solution that includes services, such as engineering support, designed to help customers answer questions, particularly in the early stages of implementation. Astute sales professionals must consider and incorporate these costs into the final price described in the business proposal made to their customers if profitability is to be maximized during the product's post-sale implementation and support phases.

For example, if the engineering support costs \$120 per hour and the average length of time needed to service customer "A" is 45 minutes, then the cost is \$90, calculated as follows:

$$TC = \$120 \times \tfrac{3}{4} \text{ hour}$$

$$= \$90$$

WHAT IT MEANS AND POTENTIAL CHALLENGES

As Peter Drucker once famously noted, the purpose of a business is to create a customer, and marketing and innovation are the only two areas that produce results.[2] Sales management and field-sales activities certainly play a critical role in this effort since they are responsible for the daily interaction with customers. Part of marketing's role is to identify segments based on customers' needs and characteristics, to target the segments that are likely to yield maximum profits, and to develop a unique position for the product or service that is relevant to the target audience. The role of the sales force is to develop ongoing business from each customer that yields positive and profitable results. Ensuring that customers are profitable is often perceived as a pricing tactic. Focusing solely on pricing is one-dimensional because it minimizes or even ignores add-on features such as product enhancements, additional service or training. Pricing strategies are designed partly to help position products (and recover costs, at a minimum). Differentiation strategies enable customers to understand why a company's products are distinctive. TDABC allows sales management to understand the indirect costs that go toward supporting and communicating the pricing and differentiation strategies they have employed.

Top sales professionals recognize that their responsibility is to convince customers to buy products and services at top prices to maximize profitability rather than resorting to discounts to secure customer commitments. Of course, the company-customer relationship is more complex than simply having sales convince customers of the merits of a full-price purchase. Strategic discounts are often built into different size commitments from customers. But the key point is that sales professionals must develop a profitable and lasting relationship with their customers.

While the enterprise-software example we used is simplistic, the lesson is powerful and useful in helping sales management understand the impact their customer relationships have on the true profits resulting from each customer. Kaplan's approach can help companies reveal previously unknown drivers of poor customer profitability. For example, while a customer's purchase of the company's products may be growing, that does not necessarily mean that profits are increasing. The cost to service that customer may have increased as well, perhaps as a result of giving in to the temptation to add product features or services to keep the customer from defecting to a competitor. Yet the additional cost to support those services and features is not captured by a corresponding increase in prices, resulting in reduced profitability.

To understand customer profitability, it is important to know all costs, not just those that are fixed. TDABC is a useful approach for identifying the specific indirect costs of each activity related to creating that customer in the first place.

Endnotes

[1] Kaplan, Robert S., "A Balanced Scorecard Approach To Measure Customer Profitability", Harvard Business School Working Knowledge, August 8, 2005.

[2] Drucker, P. *The Concept of the Corporation,* Transaction Publishers; Reprint edition 1993.

Additional Reference

Davis, J. *Measuring Marketing: 103 Key Metrics Every Marketer Needs,* John Wiley & Sons (Asia) Pte Ltd., 2007.

Part Three

SALES PERFORMANCE AND REVIEW

Reviewing individual and team performance in sales is critical to determining how successful a company has been in its recent business cycle. Did the sales people meet their individual and collective goals, quotas and overall expectations? Great sales professionals want to know how they did, even if they did not achieve all of their goals. Knowing what went well and what did not enables them to be even more successful in the future.

In this section, we examine a range of metrics that enable companies to gauge their performance in the area of sales quotas and reviews.

37

Absolute Index

THE DEFINITION

The Absolute Index measures absolute (or actual) revenues for every sales unit (region, territory, office, team, individual) and compares the result to budget revenues to arrive at a performance factor. This is useful for determining overall performance and annual bonus awards.

THE FORMULA AND ITS COMPONENTS[1]

$$AI = \frac{R_{at}}{R_{bt}}$$

Where

AI = absolute index
R_{at} = actual revenues during time period t
R_{bt} = budgeted revenues during time period t

WHERE'S THE DATA?

The data for budgeted revenues is found in the annual sales plan, which will have goals for each performance area (revenues, profits, units sold, number of accounts…). End-of-year actual-revenue figures will be part of the company's annual report. Each territory's results are unlikely to be in the annual report, but will be contained in territory-by-territory summaries provided by sales management to the finance or accounting people.

CALCULATING IT

Revenue estimates are a key target set by sales management and are derived from the company's overall performance objectives for the year. During the annual performance review, sales management compares actual revenue results to estimates.

For example, let's assume a company has five sales offices in Japan, and each is allocated an equal share of the estimated revenue target. If the total revenue target is $100 million, then each office would be responsible for generating $20 million in revenues. At the end of the year, actual revenues total $120 million. The company's absolute index is calculated as follows:

$$AI = \frac{\$120 \text{ million}}{\$100 \text{ million}}$$

$$= 1.2$$

The AI can then be broken down by territory, as shown in Figure 37.1.

Figure 37.1   Calculation of AI by territory

TERRITORY	Estimated Revenues	Actual Revenues	Absolute Index
A	$20,000,000	$26,000,000	1.3
B	$20,000,000	$17,000,000	0.85
C	$20,000,000	$24,000,000	1.2
D	$20,000,000	$28,000,000	1.4
E	$20,000,000	$25,000,000	1.25

This summary provides sales management with performance results that determine the level of bonus, if any, that is awarded.

WHAT IT MEANS AND POTENTIAL CHALLENGES

Sales performance can be measured by individual and group performances and the AI is a simple and effective tool for this purpose. Bonus awards differ for every company, but one approach is to pay a bonus equivalent to one month's salary if the sales representative achieves 100% of the assigned individual sales target (an AI of 1.0). Continuing with our example, let's assume that each sales rep earns a base salary of $48,000 annually. Therefore, monthly pay equals $4,000. The bonus awarded per sales representative would be as follows:

Territory A: $4,000 × 1.3 = $5,200
Territory B: $4,000 × 0.85 = $3,400
Territory C: $4,000 × 1.2 = $4,800
Territory D: $4,000 × 1.4 = $5,600
Territory E: $4,000 × 1.25 = $5,000

Sales management must make a decision whether Territory B even deserves a bonus, since it did not achieve its target. The decision rests on many factors:

- Were there uncontrollable factors that affected Territory B's results, such as a sudden economic change in that region or a surprising new competitor with a newer, more affordable product?

- Did individual sales representatives within the territory achieve and/or exceed their individual performance and, if so, should they be rewarded?

- Was the revenue target too aggressive for the territory?

Sales management must also consider the psychological impact of their decision. For example, if Territory B is not awarded a bonus, will the sales team be demoralized, or is that even a consideration? Conversely, if a bonus is awarded, then the other territories may be resentful since it signals that management awards bonuses even for under-performance, which may lead other territories to not work as hard in the future, knowing that they will still receive a bonus. There is no one best way to address this issue. Each of these questions and challenges must be weighed in the context of each company's unique competitive circumstances and in relation to its own company culture.

Endnote

[1] Cotte, J. and A. Yang. "Worldwide Equipment (China) Ltd: A Sales Performance Dilemma", Richard Ivey School of Business, University of Western Ontario, case # 902A28.

Relative Index

THE DEFINITION

The Relative Index (RI) measures the revenue results for each sales territory in relation to each other. It is figured once the Absolute Index (Magic Number 37) has been calculated.

THE FORMULA AND ITS COMPONENTS[1]

RI is a relative-ranking methodology, not a formula, and is determined by comparing sales territories within a country or a region based on a common performance measure, usually revenues (although it can be profits or units, depending on the company and industry).

WHERE'S THE DATA?

Similar to Magic Number 37, the performance of each territory is contained in territory-by-territory summaries provided by sales management.

CALCULATING IT

Sales management rank the final performances from best to worst to determine the RI. In our example in Magic Number 37, the respective performances of the company's five territories were as follows:

To ascertain the relative index, the territories would be ranked according to their individual performance as follows:

If sales management wish to award overall team bonuses, then RI is a helpful guide. The actual bonus amount depends on each company's

Figure 38.1   Absolute index, by territory

TERRITORY	Estimated Revenues	Actual Revenues	Absolute Index
A	$20,000,000	$26,000,000	1.3
B	$20,000,000	$17,000,000	0.85
C	$20,000,000	$24,000,000	1.2
D	$20,000,000	$28,000,000	1.4
E	$20,000,000	$25,000,000	1.25

Figure 38.2   Ranking by relative index

TERRITORY	Estimated Revenues	Actual Revenues	Absolute Index	Relative Index Rank
D	$20,000,000	$28,000,000	1.4	1
A	$20,000,000	$26,000,000	1.3	2
E	$20,000,000	$25,000,000	1.25	3
C	$20,000,000	$24,000,000	1.2	4
B	$20,000,000	$17,000,000	0.85	5

real situation, but for illustration we will assume that the five territories were required to meet their target before a bonus is paid. Furthermore, since there are five territories, we will assume that the RI-based team bonus generously awards five times the base bonus to the top team, four times to the second-ranked team, three times to the third-ranked team, twice to the fourth-ranked team, and one time to the fifth-ranked team. Clearly, this structure has its fiduciary limits since a company with 50 sales territories would pay enormous sums to the top teams, so a more-sophisticated model would be used, but the evaluation process would remain the same.

The bonus awarded per sales representative would then be as follows:

Territory D: $4,000 \times 1.4 = $5,600 \times 5 = $28,000

Territory A: $4,000 \times 1.3 = $5,200 \times 4 = $20,800

Territory E: $4,000 \times 1.25 = $5,000 \times 3 = $15,000$

Territory C: $4,000 \times 1.2 \ = $4,800 \times 2 = $9,600$

Territory B: $4,000 \times 0.85 = $3,400 \times 1 = $3,400$

WHAT IT MEANS AND POTENTIAL CHALLENGES

The RI is effective with almost any sales criteria since it is merely a ranking methodology, with the stipulation that the figures used to determine the relative rankings must be consistent (i.e. use only revenues, or units, or profits, for example).

Magic Number 37, from which RI is derived, illustrated the impact of each territory's AI on the bonus awarded. Here, we showed that Territory B's sales representatives each received a bonus of $3,400. However, most companies are unlikely to pay bonuses when targets are not met, unless the circumstances are extraordinary.

Endnote

[1] Cotte, J. and A. Yang, "Worldwide Equipment (China) Ltd: A Sales Performance Dilemma", Richard Ivey School of Business, University of Western Ontario, case # 902A28 pp. 9–10.

39 Sales Performance Quotas

The Definition

Sales volume quotas are minimum performance goals set by sales management for each sales representative. Quotas are a common tool for companies of all sizes because they guide sales people on where to apply their effort, motivate them to perform, and serve as benchmark standards for evaluating performance.

The Formula and Its Components[1]

The following information can provide useful guidelines for establishing sales volume quotas:

- The previous year's total company or territory sales numbers, by product or customer

- The previous year's individual sales person's sales numbers, by product or customer

- Sales costs with a multiplier ($\times 3$, for example). A sales cost multiplier is a metric used by management to ensure that, at a minimum, the sales representative earns more than he or she spends to attract business. Management determine the multiplier based on historical costs for attracting customers

- Corporate general administrative costs plus a gross margin

- Revenue goals committed to industry analysts or shareholders

- Total of the sales team's goals (by territory, product or customer) divided by the number of sales people

- Estimated income potential provided to individual sales staff if they achieve their quota

- Analyst's projected annual growth rate for the industry for the current year (for example, if the analyst forecasts industry growth of 20%, then quotas are up 20%)

- Sales management's experiences at other companies, since sales managers and sales executives will have familiarity working with sales organizations, including quota development.

WHERE'S THE DATA?

The quota data is derived from the items listed above.

CALCULATING IT

To illustrate the first point listed above, let's look at the sales revenues by quarter for Procter & Gamble in 2005,[2] as shown in Figure 39.1.

Figure 39.1   Sales revenues for Procter & Gamble, 2003

PERIOD ENDING 2005	31-Dec-05	30-Sep-05	30-Jun-05	31-Mar-05
Total Revenue	18,337,000	14,793,000	14,258,000	14,287,000

If Procter & Gamble were to use volume quotas to guide its sales people, then these quarterly revenue figures would be further divided by region and/or product group and/or customer type. The sales representatives would receive a quota for 2006 based on these figures from 2005, plus percentage increases described by the company's growth plan for 2006. This example uses dollars as the standard measure.

WHAT IT MEANS AND POTENTIAL CHALLENGES

Sales management establish quotas that serve as revenue targets for each sales representative. The quotas apply to one or more growth objectives — geographic territories, product sales and/or number of customers — and are measured in dollars or units.

The sales-management plan flows directly from the corporate strategic plan and key marketing objectives. For example, the corporate strategic plan may set product innovation as the primary objective. Marketing would develop its customer-development plans based on this objective. In this case, it would target early-adopter customers who find innovative products appealing. Sales would then identify specific customers who are the closest fit to the corporate and marketing profiles. When the targets are achieved, sales representatives receive compensation above and beyond their base salary.

Planning assumptions are important when developing sales quotas. Reflecting on the Procter & Gamble (P&G) example, if the company does set future quotas based on the previous year's sales plus percentage increases based on the company growth plan, then it assumes that the sales staff have maximized the potential of their respective markets the previous year. In Figure 39.2 below, the sales person exceeded the one-year target of $1.2 million by $150,000, achieving 113% of the assigned quota.

Figure 39.2   Measuring individual performance against target

Quota	One-year target	Actual	Quota % achieved
Sales Volume ($)	$1,200,000	$1,350,000	113%

However, the sales person may be an under-performer in a territory with significant potential. Therefore, using the previous year's performance plus expected growth may still not realize the full potential of the territory. Sales management must work directly with the sales representative to develop quotas based on the territory's true potential.

Sales quotas are most effective when sales people are directly involved with sales management in developing goals. Setting goals with management allows sales staff to give and receive direct feedback on their past performances, and provide insights into the unique characteristics of their territory.

Individual sales quotas are less effective in team-selling situations since cooperation may be hindered by each sales person's individual performance goals. Team quotas are feasible, but require a clear agreement among the team members that success is based on their combined efforts, irrespective of imbalances in individual contribution. However, contribution imbalances are likely since each person has a different point of view on how best to achieve an objective. Team quotas may therefore be short-lived since one or more members of the team may feel they are being under-compensated for their contribution. Sales volume quotas are less effective with large-scale industrial sales such as heavy equipment or complex enterprise software because the sales cycles are unpredictable and quite long. Products with extreme pricing variation are harder to measure in this way since market conditions may make early planning assumptions invalid at the time of the actual sale. Ultimately, sales volume quotas reward activities related to selling. Non-selling activities such as planning, proposal development and customer-support programs are usually ignored.

Addendum 1: The unit-volume quota

The performance expectations of sales representatives selling high-cost products such as computer hardware, complex enterprise software or products with significant pricing variation are measured more effectively with a unit-volume quota.

For example, if a sales person sells 50 units of a product priced at $10,000 per unit, then $500,000 is the total sales figure. But if the price increases 20%, to $12,000 per unit (perhaps the cost of materials increases), then only 42 units are sold at the same dollar volume.

If the objective of the sales person is to sell 50 units, then the challenge is to achieve that target irrespective of price. A unit-volume quota shifts the emphasis to features and benefits that solve the customer's problem so that price becomes secondary. It also forces a change in the sales person's behavior. In Addendum 4 we will discuss activity quotas, which establish performance goals for activities related to improved performance in revenues, profits, market share, product volume, territory development or customer acquisition, and retention.

Addendum 2: The point-quota system

Point-quota systems set targets based on accumulating a certain number of points, rather than dollars or units. Point quotas reward sales representatives for selling certain combinations of products, dollar volumes or units. For example, to encourage new-product placement, sales management may award five points for new products, three points for upgrades and two points for legacy products. Management may also award points for certain levels of dollar or unit sales achieved. Or, they might convert new-product, dollar and unit sales into points.

Point systems are useful when management wants to change the behavior of sales representatives who are meeting their quotas through the sale of one or two key products that are easier to sell, downplaying other products as a result. Senior management would assign more points to products that need greater placement in the market. Alternatively, if profitability needs to be improved, then points can be assigned to those products with higher relative profitability.

To illustrate, let's look at a variation of the example used earlier and assume that P&G's management wish to improve sales of products "A" and "B" because they are more profitable than products "C" and "D", which are less profitable but easier to sell. Furthermore, P&G decides to award one bonus point for any sales above quota. Figure 39.3 below shows the respective performances of two sales reps.

Figure 39.3   The point-quota system illustrated

Sales Rep 1				
Quota	One-year point target	Actual	Quota % achieved	Bonus points
Product A	5	6	120%	1
Product B	4	5	125%	1
Product C	3	4	133%	1
Product D	3	3	100%	0
			119.5%	3
Sales Rep 2				
Quota	One-year point target	Actual	Quota % achieved	Bonus points
Product A	5	4	80%	0
Product B	4	2	50%	0
Product C	3	2	300%	0
Product D	3	9	200%	1
			157.5%	2

In the point system, senior management will reward the first sales rep more favorably than the second rep, even though the second achieved 157.5% of quota, as opposed to the first sales rep's 119.5%. The first sales rep earned her bonus by beating her quota with the harder-to-sell products that are also more profitable.

Point-quota systems have the advantage of forcing the sales team to focus on products that management are seeking to sell, but the disadvantage of having to deal with growing complexity as a company's product offering expands into multiple lines and product pricing levels.

Addendum 3: The profit quota

Where the point-quota system helps focus sales attention on management's product-mix priorities, the profit quota pushes sales representatives to achieve pre-determined profits for each product's sales volume. Profits are defined on the basis of either a gross margin or a contribution margin. Gross margin is the difference between net sales (gross sales minus returns, discounts and allowances) and the cost of goods sold (expenses associated with producing the product, including labor, raw material and overheads). Contribution margin is defined as the sales price minus the variable costs. The profit-quota approach works best when sales representatives have some influence over final pricing. P&G's actual 2005 gross margin was over 52%, so the profit quota would set a gross margin target of at least 52% for each product. In our earlier example, products "A" and "B" have higher profits; therefore, management might set a gross margin target of 60%. Products "C" and "D" might have a gross margin target of 48%. The goal is to meet or exceed each gross margin target. If this is done, then a bonus is paid.

Addendum 4: The activity quota

Companies set performance targets that include specific financial, market and product objectives. These objectives are translated into specific targets for particular areas of the business. Sales people are rewarded according to their individual performance in achieving the specific targets set for them. Senior management need a tool that motivates sales people to pursue the right activities so that the goals are reached. Activity quotas are a good tool for motivating sales staff to plan the specific activities that will lead to improved performance in their territory.

Sales management must establish activity quotas that set proper expectations for their sales team. Activity quotas include:

- Total number of calls to new and existing customers per period of time

- Total number of letters sent to prospective customers

- New account calls

- Product displays

- Account meetings with loyal customers

- Presentations to customers on additional product and support services

- Internal account-update meetings

- Coordinating product installations

- Account coordination meetings with strategic partners

- New proposals.

Activity quotas are intended to guide specific behaviors that will ensure that performance targets are met. Sales management must define the most important activities their sales representatives perform, from which specific activity targets are then set. If the right behaviors and activities are identified and measured, then sales people should have a clear picture of senior management's expectations and an equally clear sense of those activities that do not conform to those expectations and should, therefore, be avoided.

In Figure 39.4 below, the rep achieved 113% of the set sales-volume quota. Table E illustrates how activity quotas can provide a clearer picture of the sales representative's performance.

Figure 39.4   Activity quotas for assessing individual performance

Quota	One-year target	Actual	Quota % achieved
Sales Volume	$1,200,000	$1,350,000	113%
Product demonstrations	24	18	75%
Average calls per week	30	24	80%
New accounts per month	5	4	80%
		Average	87%

Sales management would review this performance with the rep to improve the weaker activity areas. Since the sales-volume quota was exceeded while the other activity areas under-performed, they would want to establish more aggressive sales-volume targets as well.

Whether activity quotas have been achieved is determined from the sales call reports of each sales representative, which places responsibility on the sales person to keep accurate records of the results of meetings with customers. Sales management may occasionally audit the data from these reports by calling the customers to verify the information. However, audits can send a de-motivating signal that conveys a lack of trust between sales management and the sales representatives.

Each quota system in this chapter provides management with a method for achieving a particular result. However, setting quotas is complex since most businesses do not face uniform markets with consistent customer demands and clearly delineated offerings from competitors. Therefore, companies may employ multiple quota methods for the same product simply to take account of differences across territories. Each sales rep's territory is likely to differ in any number of ways, including:

- Maturity of the local market

- Popularity and reputation of the company's products vis-à-vis those of the competition

- Number of qualified customers

- Economic characteristics of each market

- Sales potential of each territory

- Financial targets for each territory.

Finally, even with sound quota systems, the performance of each sales representative also depends on "softer" abilities such as motivation, confidence and desire. Setting quotas for these intangibles is not possible, but their influence in successful selling is well-researched and should be carefully factored into each rep's individual performance plan.

Endnotes

[1] Adapted from http://www.derbymanagement.com/knowledge/pages/tactics/setting1.html

[2] http://finance.yahoo.com/q/is?s=PG

Additional References

Davis, J. *Measuring Marketing: 103 Key Metrics Every Marketer Needs,* John Wiley & Sons (Asia) Pte Ltd., 2007.

http://www.buseco.monash.edu.au/depts/mkt/dictionary/uuu.php

http://en.mimi.hu/marketingweb/unit_volume_quota.html

http://rcw.raifoundation.org/management/mba/saleanddistributionmgmt/lecture-notes/lecture-19.pdf

http://www.marketingpower.com/mdictionary.php?Searched=1&SearchFor=quota&Term_ID=3805&SearchDefinitionsAlso=ON

Average Sales Per Call

The Definition[1]

Average sales per call measures the value in dollar sales arising from each sales call made by each sales person.

The Formula and Its Components

The formula for this metric is:

$$SPC_{avg} = \frac{T_{salest}}{T_{callst}}$$

Where

SPC_{avg} = average sales per call
T_{salest} = total sales in time period t
T_{callst} = total calls in time period t

Where's the Data?

The source data comes from total sales generated in a given period of time and the total number of calls made during that same period. The data is not composed of hypothetical figures, but actual results, and sales management can use either individual or team totals in calculating sales per call. Industry comparisons can be made, assuming reliable data is available, but most companies do not reveal these figures for competitive reasons. Experienced sales professionals will have informal data (market intelligence) from their ongoing activities in the field, where customers may reveal a competitor's information, or even competitors themselves may casually describe the general sales figures from their efforts. These are not common nor precisely reliable sources, but the combination of informal and formal sources will help sales representatives determine if their performance is similar to others in the same industry.

CALCULATING IT

Woodside Hotels is a small, upscale hotel company based in Northern California. The sales team consists of two sales people for each of the five properties belonging to the company. Each sales person is responsible for group business (ten or more rooms for each group). Most of the sales people conduct their own customer research and cold calling (there is no telemarketing or third-party market-research firm to help). The average number of sales calls (cold calls included) in a five-day work week is 75, and the average total group sales per sales rep per week is $20,000. Therefore, the average sales per call is calculated as follows:

$$SPC_{avg} = \frac{\$20,000}{75}$$
$$= \$267$$

Each call generates $267 in revenue.

WHAT IT MEANS AND POTENTIAL CHALLENGES

A quick review of these numbers will suggest that not every sales call results in revenue being generated. Instead, only a few of each week's 75 calls lead to group bookings, usually four or five. Assuming five bookings is the average number of bookings per week, then the average sales per booking call is $4,000, a more reasonable result given the price of rooms, length of stay and size of groups.

This metric helps sales management understand each sales person's performance, both individually and compared to other sales people. Over time and repeated measuring, performance patterns will emerge that will guide future sales-management decisions on customer-account management, territory structure, pricing latitude and target segments. Knowing the average sales per call will also help sales management understand the strengths and weaknesses of each sales person with respect to the kinds of customers being contacted, thereby aligning account assignments more effectively in the future.

As a stand-alone measure, average sales per call is less revealing than if it is applied in conjunction with other productivity measures, based on company goals.

References

Davis, J. *Measuring Marketing: 103 Key Metrics Every Marketer Needs,* John Wiley & Sons (Asia) Pte Ltd., 2007.
http://www.referenceforbusiness.com/encyclopedia/res-sec/sales-management.html
http://www.exinfm.com/workshop_files/sales_customer_measures.doc

41 Close Process and Close Ratio

THE DEFINITION

The close process describes the effort expended by the sales representative to secure a purchase commitment from the customer. Each step of the entire sales cycle, from identification of the customer to cold calling to meetings with the customer to completing the sale, brings the sales rep closer to closing the sale. But the final stages, after customers have agreed that the sales person's offering is attractive, are often the most challenging because customers may be considering similar products from competitors. The final decision may come down to factors outside the sales person's control, despite a winning business proposition that seems to meet the customer's needs.

The close ratio describes the number of deals closed as a proportion of the total number of customers in the sales cycle (also called the "sales pipeline").

THE FORMULA AND ITS COMPONENTS

The close process

Historically, there are several known variations on the typical sales cycle, including AICP (awareness, interest, conviction, purchase) and AICTR (awareness, interest, conviction, trial, repeat).

As sales techniques have grown in sophistication, so too has the close process and, consequently, the steps involved in the time to close. This process is represented in Figure 41.1.[1]

Figure 41.1   Common steps in the sales process

	Target 0%	Qualify 16%	Meet & Greet 25%	Present 50%	Proposal 60%	Due Diligence 80%	Pending Sale 95%	Close 100%
I N T E R E S T	Brochures Data Sheets Website Internet Research	ROI Needs-Analysis Survey White Paper Case Studies	ROI Needs-Analysis Survey Competitor Analysis Partner Profiles	ROI Needs-Analysis Survey Pre-Sales Engineers Manager Visit	ROI Needs-Analysis Survey Financial Dashboard Proposal Dept.	Impact Study Market Reference Checklist 360 degree ROI Statistics	Legal Dept.	

The chart shows the common steps in the sales process, from initial targeting to close. Each step is labeled across the top of the horizontal axis and the accompanying percentage indicates the likelihood of the sale being concluded at that stage. Within each step are many of the probable activities that occur in that stage. The percentages and activities listed are purely for illustration and each sales-management team and rep will have a better understanding of what is required in each stage to meet their particular needs. The bell curve illustrates the intensity of effort, which reaches its peak in the presentation and proposal stages, where a great deal of effort goes into preparing these critical phases. Assuming the customer remains interested, the sales effort shifts toward concluding the sale (and minimizing any last-minute obstacles). The trailing off of the curve at this stage does not imply that the sales person loses interest as the sale approaches the close phase. It merely reflects the changing intensity of effort, rather than a diminishing of interest.

The close ratio

At any given time, a sales person will have multiple customers, each at different stages of the close process. In the early stages, the sales people either cold call customers themselves, or calls are made on their behalf by the company's telemarketing team. Through this process they identify and separate those customers worth pursuing from those no longer of interest. Not all customers will complete the cycle. As the sales person and customer move through the stages, they each increase their commitment to the effort and reduce the chances of there being a cancellation before the close. The sales person and sales management are interested in the percentage of customers that close once they enter the close-process cycle. This is expressed as follows:

$$CR_t = \frac{C_{at}}{C_{pt}} \times 100$$

Where

CR_t = close ratio in time period t
C_{at} = actual sales closed in time period t
C_{pt} = potential sales to close in time period t

WHERE'S THE DATA?

The data for potential sales comes from the sales plan, which is developed at the beginning of each planning and budget cycle, usually annually. The sales plan enumerates company goals, which are translated into regional, local and account goals. The actual data on the number of sales closed is based on end-of-period reports that summarize the actual business earned. The actual data is summarized in the corporate financial and accounting statements.

CALCULATING IT

Let's assume that a sales person for a medical-devices company has 12 potential customers per month over the course of a year. On average, seven customers per month complete the process to close. This sales person's close ratio is thus calculated as follows:

$$CR_t = \frac{84}{144} \times 100$$
$$= 58\%$$

WHAT IT MEANS AND POTENTIAL CHALLENGES

The sales person is interested in closing sales as quickly as possible and with maximum financial benefit to himself and the company (see Magic Numbers 17–23 for more information on different incentive structures to reward specific performance objectives). Sales management also want to evaluate each sales person's performance.

The close process is important as it helps sales staff plan their progress toward the close and, psychologically, it helps them see the progress, providing a form of motivation. Sales reps who are experts in their industry and understand their customers are quite likely to be able to estimate the probable length of time required for each stage of the cycle. The process also enables them to know the current standing of each of their customers, which in turn helps them to organize their work effort more effectively, including mapping out which buyers need to be contacted at a particular stage of the process. (B2B sales efforts, for example, usually involve buying teams, with each person having a different interest.) The best sales people keep detailed notes of each meeting with the customer so they can identify gaps in their selling efforts, to be addressed at the next meeting.

The close ratio ultimately measures their success in the close process. Returning to the earlier example, if the sales person were able to improve the close ratio to eight out of 12 potentials each month, the improvement in their close ratio is significant, and they have gained 12 additional customers during that same time period, which will improve their future repeat sales business:

$$CR_t = \frac{96}{144} \times 100$$
$$= 67\%$$

By using the close process and close ratio together, the sales rep can more easily identify stages where potential business is lost, and use this information to improve their own future sales results and income, and the company's business.

Endnote

[1] Koenig, K. M. and M. J. Nick. *ROI Selling,* Dearborn Trade Books, 2004: p. 250.

Additional References

Cron, W. L., T. E. DeCarlo and D. J. Palrymple. *Sales Management*, John Wiley & Sons, Inc., 2004: pp. 215–218.

Davis, J. *Measuring Marketing: 103 Key Metrics Every Marketer Needs*, John Wiley & Sons (Asia) Pte Ltd., 2007.

Doyle, C. *Collins Internet-Linked Dictionary of Marketing*, Harper Collins, 2003, 2006: p. 70.

Imber, J. and B. A. Toffler, *Dictionary of Marketing Terms*, Barron's Educational Series, 2000: p. 108.

42 Cost Per Call

THE DEFINITION

Cost per call measures the total amount spent for every call made to customers. It helps sales management determine the cost-effectiveness of each dollar of revenue generated.

THE FORMULA AND ITS COMPONENTS

To determine cost per call, the sales person needs three pieces of data:

- Sales expenses per time period (usually one year)
- Total number of selling days in that period
- Average number of calls per day.

WHERE'S THE DATA?

The sales-expenses data is based on historical expenses, with greater emphasis assigned to more recent time periods. If a company's sales force is new (perhaps previously the company's products were sold by an independent sales agency, or online), then historical data may be insignificant or non-existent. In this case, data can be acquired through a market-research firm or industry trade publications.

The total number of selling days in the chosen time period will vary by company because of differences in vacation policies, training days, time required for internal meetings and similar non-selling activities. Sales management will need to determine the total selling days for each person in their sales force if an accurate, individual measure is required. While totaling all sales days and dividing by the number of sales people will produce an average, it will not reflect the specific selling and non-selling schedules of individual sales representatives.

The data for the average number of calls per day can be gathered at the individual sales representative or team sales levels. If an average without regard for specific individual performance is required, the total number of calls made by the team divided by the number of team members in that time period will provide that information. But accurate individual performance reviews will require sales management to calculate each individual representative's performance.

CALCULATING IT

According to *Sales & Marketing Management* magazine, the average compensation (base salary plus bonus and commissions) for all sales people in the United States in 2003 was US$111,135.[1] This figure is only part of the total sales expense, however. Sales people incur additional expenses in the course of their annual selling activities, including those associated with transportation, entertainment and support materials. The number of actual selling days is affected by non-selling demands on their time, including training, meetings, vacations and weekends. Sales professionals must budget for each of these components when forecasting their total selling expenses if they want an accurate estimate of their cost per call. Figure 42.1 captures these additional figures[2] for an individual sales person and shows a cost per call of $270.80.

WHAT IT MEANS AND POTENTIAL CHALLENGES

Sales professionals must grow the business by finding new customers and getting existing customers to buy more products. Therefore, they must allocate their limited time toward the best customer prospects. However, sales people need to know how much their time is worth and the expense of making contact with each customer, so they need to calculate their cost per call.

Top sales performers succeed because they plan their activities rigorously to maximize selling time to the right customers. Measuring cost per call enables sales people to determine the costs incurred to make each sales call. Cost per call is a useful tool in the beginning of any sales plan because it forces the sales person to think carefully about the many expenses incurred in pursuit of each sale. However, it is just

Figure 42.1   Calculating cost per call, incorporating additional factors

COMPENSATION		
Salary, commissions, bonus	$111,135	
Fringe benefits (insurance and other)	$15,225	$126,360
DIRECT SELLING EXPENSES		
Automobile	$12,636	
Lodging and meals	$9,856	
Entertainment	$5,181	
Communications	$7,076	
Samples, promotional materials	$2,780	
Miscellaneous	$2,654	$40,183
Total Direct Expenses		$166,543
CALLS PER YEAR		
Total available days		260 days
Less:		
Vacation	10 days	
Holidays	10 days	
Sickness	5 days	
Meetings	18 days	
Training	12 days	55 days
Net selling days		205 days
Average calls per day		3 calls
Total calls per year (205 × 3)	615 calls	
Average cost per call ($166,543/615)		$270.80

one of several key planning steps. The following Magic Numbers add depth to the sales planning effort.

Endnotes

[1] Galea, C. "2004 Salary Survey", *Sales & Marketing Management*, May 2004: p. 28.
[2] Adapted from: Cron, W. L., T. E. DeCarlo and D. J. Palrymple, *Sales Management*. John Wiley & Sons, Inc., 2004: p. 127.

Additional Reference

Davis, J. *Measuring Marketing: 103 Key Metrics Every Marketer Needs,* John Wiley & Sons (Asia) Pte Ltd., 2007.

43 Break-Even Sales Volume

THE DEFINITION

The break-even point is the minimum sale needed for revenues to equal costs. Any sale below break-even should be avoided.

THE FORMULA AND ITS COMPONENTS[1]

The formula for break-even sales volume is common across industries, although the formula's variables will vary, sometimes dramatically, by industry and even within an industry.

$$BE_{sv} = \frac{CPC \times NCC}{Cs}$$

Where

BE_{sv} = break-even sales volume in dollars
CPC = cost per call
NCC = number of calls to close
Cs   = sales costs, expressed as a percentage of sales

WHERE'S THE DATA?

"Cost per call" data was described in detail in Magic Number 42, but the information is derived from:

- Sales expenses per time period

- Total number of selling days per time period

- Average number of calls per day.

The number of calls to close is based on recent historical data describing the number of times the sales person had to meet (or talk via phone or email) the customer before the sale was completed.

The sales costs data is determined from total expenses incurred in the selling effort. The costs are divided by the total number of sales representatives during the same time period to determine an average. Alternatively, sales management can calculate sales costs for each sales person. While this is more time-consuming, it is also more accurate since the answer reflects a more accurate individual review of each sales representative.

CALCULATING IT

There are no universal rules governing the number of calls required to close a sale. Selling consumer perishables, such as canned foods, is very different from selling mainframe computers. The canned-foods sales person may be able to close a sale in two or three calls since the buyer regularly needs to replenish inventory on store shelves. The mainframe computer sales person may have several meetings over several months with the buyers before a sale is concluded. Sales people should be familiar with the performance standards of their industry. Their own experience with customers also serves as a relevant guideline for the number of calls typically needed to close a sale. Even with industries where practices tend to be similar overall, each company within the industry is quite likely to allocate percentages differently for each expense category, including direct selling expenses. Sales people must learn management's expectations and factor these into their break-even analysis. Figure 43.1 shows actual percentages by industry.[2]

Using the chart, each industry's break-even sales volume can be calculated. To illustrate, let's look at food products:

$$BE_{sv} = \frac{\$131.60 \times 4.8}{0.027}$$
$$= \$23,396$$

The sales staff now have a minimum performance benchmark that helps them target customers more effectively, reallocating time and resources away from customers who do not meet the standard.

Figure 43.1 Calculating break-even sales volume: cross-industry comparisons

Industry	Cost per call (in $)	No. of calls needed to close a sale	Sales costs as a % age of total sales
Business services	46.00	4.6	10.3%
Chemicals	165.80	2.8	3.4
Construction	111.20	2.8	7.1
Electronics	133.30	3.9	12.6
Food products	131.60	4.8	2.7
Instruments	226.00	5.3	14.8
Machinery	68.50	3.0	11.3
Office equipment	25.00	3.7	2.4
Printing/publishing	70.10	4.5	22.2
Rubber/plastic	248.20	4.7	3.6

WHAT IT MEANS AND POTENTIAL CHALLENGES

In Magic Number 42 we saw how to calculate cost per call. Figuring the break-even sales volume helps sales people determine the best customer or sales size (by dollars).

Successful sales planning requires sales managers and their team members to evaluate their customers carefully. The minimum performance benchmarks are not hard-and-fast rules, since an under-performing customer may have potential to be brought above break-even.

The break-even sales volume provides a minimum acceptable standard for determining the attractiveness of a customer account. The measure helps sales people focus on those businesses that represent the best potential, reducing the number of less-attractive customers. They can then begin the more rigorous phases of their account planning, including profiling each account and the main buyers in greater detail. However, business decisions are usually more complex than this simple illustration. A customer may be below the break-even threshold, yet if their business is growing at an attractive rate (for example, ahead of the pace of their competitors), then management should consider the longer-term potential before dropping them. There may also be inefficiencies in the sales company's system which, upon correction, may change the break-even calculation and allow more customers to survive. New products may also change the relationship with customers, who may find the new offerings attractive. Even though the break-even threshold is not met, the customer's previously profitable loyalty may suggest that the overall relationship should be nurtured, despite the initially unattractive break-even volumes for the new product.

Sales professionals have many factors to consider when reviewing their customers. Calculating break-even sales volume is a logical step to take since it helps focus the sales effort, improving efficiency (the wrong accounts won't be pursued) and effectiveness (the sales person now knows the sales amount required to break even). The challenge arises from the complexity of other factors that cannot be easily measured, such as long-term potential and ease of servicing a particular account, yet can have a significant impact on success over the long term.

Endnotes

[1] Adapted from: Cron, W. L., T. E. DeCarlo and D. J. Palrymple, *Sales Management.* John Wiley & Sons, Inc., 2004: pp. 126–127.
[2] Ibid: p. 128.

Additional References

Davis, J. *Measuring Marketing: 103 Key Metrics Every Marketer Needs,* John Wiley & Sons (Asia) Pte Ltd., 2007.
Doyle, C. *Collins Internet-Linked Dictionary of Marketing,* Harper Collins, 2003, 2006: pp.45–47.
Imber, J. and B. A. Toffler, *Dictionary of Marketing Terms,* Barron's Educational Series, 2000: p.71.
http://www.toolkit.cch.com/text/P06_7530.asp
http://www.ces.purdue.edu/extmedia/EC/EC-725.pdf

Sales Productivity

THE DEFINITION

Sales productivity simply describes how productive sales people are. Productivity can be measured in the following ways:

- Sales (revenues) per person (measured in dollars)

- Profits per person (measured in dollars)

- Volume sold per person (in units).

Most productivity measures focus on revenues per person.

THE FORMULA AND ITS COMPONENTS

$$SP = \frac{\Sigma S_t}{\Sigma S_p}$$

Where

SP = sales productivity
ΣS_t = sum of total sales for all sales people
ΣS_p = total number of sales people

WHERE'S THE DATA?

Sales management will have total sales figures from performance summaries for each period of time being measured. These figures are sent on to the company's accounting or finance departments and included in the overall financial review of the business. While sales management's numbers should be accurate, the finance department has final information on returned products after the sale, customer discounts and similar allowances or reimbursements, which affects the final sales total.

Sales management, human resources, and finance should each have the data on the total number of sales people, although sales management is most likely to have the up-to-date information.

CALCULATING IT

In the 1990s, Transamerica Intellitech was a small U.S.-based company that sold real-estate data and software to title companies, real-estate firms, appraisers and financial institutions. In 1996, the company's revenues were $11 million, generated by 33 sales people. Thus, sales productivity was as follows:

$$SP = \frac{\$11,000,000}{33}$$

$$= \$333,334 \text{ per person}$$

The data was hard to verify, but management's evaluation suggested that the average sales productivity of the company's competitors was at least double that of Transamerica Intellitech. The senior management team embarked on an aggressive growth plan that included new products and acquisitions. By 1999, revenues had grown to $42 million and the sales team numbered 60. Sales productivity changed as well:

$$SP = \frac{\$42,000,000}{60}$$

$$= \$700,000 \text{ per person}$$

Clearly, sales productivity per person improved during that period of time. This provided a key performance measure enabling management to evaluate sales progress more effectively.

WHAT IT MEANS AND POTENTIAL CHALLENGES

Sales productivity is a simple measure as used here. The results of this analysis will affect decisions at the company, team and individual levels. Since every company's needs differ, measures of productivity will vary accordingly. Every company's leadership should develop its own productivity measures, derived from the business-plan goals. Measuring sales productivity should inspire deeper analysis of the underlying causes of the performance (whether good or bad). Decision making will focus more on the detailed questions raised by the sales-productivity results, which are affected by overall company goals, sales targets, sales territory definition, and segment and account strategies.

Company-level decisions are complicated by hard-to-control factors. Assuming sales managers are familiar with their teams, they may conclude that a poor performance as revealed by sales-productivity analysis could be due to other, less-controllable factors such as unrealistic goals, a weak correlation between pay and performance or shifting market conditions that affected the assumptions that supported the original sales plan. These must be weighed against sales management's future compensation plans, sales targets, account objectives and, ultimately, changes in personnel.

Sales management will use productivity to understand a sales representative's individual performance in comparison with those of colleagues or competitors. Marketing can use the results to advise under-performers about more-effective segmentation or new segment opportunities. Sales management can use the results to counsel poor performers in better account selection, time management and selling strategies for each customer. More specifically, sales managers can use the productivity results to develop a step-by-step plan for improved individual performance.

Finally, sales management must be careful not to misinterpret sales-productivity data. The performance of a handful of top performers may serve to disguise the under-performance of the rest of the team. Therefore, the results will need to be viewed across the sales force and at the individual level. High performers will certainly generate substantial revenues, but if those results are partly secured by offering customers generous, low-cost support contracts, then the financial impact on the rest of the company could be severe. Perhaps the high performers generated strong sales, but also had higher returns as a result of a less-thoughtful selling effort. Or, their significant sales volume may strain the company's production and delivery capabilities, particularly if the revenue growth is sudden and sharp. The outcome could be unhappy customers, which is certainly counter to the purpose of selling and marketing in the first place.

References

Davis, J. *Measuring Marketing: 103 Key Metrics Every Marketer Needs,* John Wiley & Sons (Asia) Pte Ltd., 2007.
http://hbswk.hbs.edu/item.jhtml?id=3952&t=dispatch
http://www.entrepreneur.com/article/0,4621,324059,00.html
http://www.exinfm.com/workshop_files/sales_customer_measures.doc

Four-Factor Model

THE DEFINITION

"Four factor" describes four criteria that are commonly used to assess the performance of sales staff.

THE FORMULA AND ITS COMPONENTS[1]

The four-factor model evaluates a sales person's efforts in four specific areas:

- Number of days worked
- Calls per days worked
- Orders/calls
- Sales $/orders.

The formula used is:

$$\$ \text{ Sales } = \text{ Days worked } \times \frac{\text{Calls}}{\text{Days worked}} \times \frac{\text{Orders}}{\text{Calls}} \times \frac{\text{Sales } \$}{\text{Orders}}$$

WHERE'S THE DATA?

The data is found in sales management's personnel files since each sales person's results are tracked for compensation and performance-review purposes. The information may also be contained in sales activity reports for each period of time being evaluated. These reports will be in both the sales management and finance/accounting departments.

Benchmark comparisons can be made against industry data as well. Industry data is found via third-party market research or industry trade publications. Finally, human resources may also have benchmark data gleaned from interviews with candidates for sales positions.

CALCULATING IT

Let's look at Northwest Resorts, Inc. (NWR),[2] a hospitality company that owns one resort and works in partnership with another six regional hotels and resorts, representing a total of 900 hotel rooms. Sales people are compensated for booking group business, defined as 10 or more rooms per night plus one group meal and two coffee breaks during the day (minimum), each day. Figure 45.1 outlines the performance of three of NWR's sales people:

Figure 45.1   Comparison of sales reps' performance

Criteria	Sales Rep 1	Sales Rep 2	Sales Rep 3
Annual sales	$622,200	$1,567,125	$931,139
Days worked	230	225	231
Total calls*	2,760	3,375	3,696
Group bookings	100	90	112
Avg. length of stay (# of nights)	2	3.5	3
Avg. daily rate per person per group	$148	$134	$90
Avg. daily F&B per person per group	$35	$65	$42
Avg. # of rooms	17	25	21
Total calls/total days worked	12	15	16
Bookings/call	3.6%	2.7%	3%
Sales $/booking	$6,222	$17,413	$8,313
Sales expense (non-wage)	$6,500	$17,200	$9,000
Sales expense per call	$2.35	$5.16	$2.43
Sales expense per booking	$65	$191.11	$80.36
Sales expense as % of total sales	1.04%	1.1%	0.97%
FOUR-FACTOR TOTAL**	**$618,218**	**$1,586,760**	**$921,745**

* calls defined as: telephone, client tours of hotels, visits to client sites. Most calls were by telephone.
** Sales Rep 1 = 230 x 12 × 0.036 × $6,222 = $618,218
Sales Rep 2 = 225 x 15 × 0.027 × $17,413 = $1,586,760
Sales Rep 3 = 231 x 16 × 0.030 × $8,313 = $921,745

What It Means and Potential Challenges

Performance appraisal of sales people is complex. Qualitative influences such as attitude, emotional resiliency and persistence play an important role in successful selling but are difficult to evaluate objectively. While achieving consistently successful sales results is never assured, certain tasks performed by sales people are clear and measurable since they are developed with a specific eye toward growth in revenues, profits, units sold and number of customers. These tasks are part of the selling routine and include setting personal goals, identifying customer targets, organizing the sales tactics for each customer, scheduling sales calls, closing sales and, finally, following up with the customer after the sale is complete. Since each of these activities yields a clear result, sales management needs a way to measure them.

The four-factor calculations in our example show dollar-sales totals nearly the same as the total annual sales for each sales person. The numbers are interesting, given the sizable differences between sales reps, but sales management will want to review the performances and their underlying causes with greater scrutiny. For example, Sales Rep 2's four-factor results are higher than her annual sales. The most obvious factor is her average sales dollars per booking. Her total dollars per group is larger because the number of rooms her groups book is substantially higher, as is the average length of stay for her groups. Before concluding that she is superior to her colleagues, however, sales management should review her territory, because the customers in her territory may be substantially larger than those of the other two. So Sales Rep 2's customers may simply book more rooms per group as a result of having more employees and, therefore, larger group-travel needs. Her typical customer's average length of stay is also longer, which may signal she is more effective at selling hotel space, perhaps by emphasizing unique features that business groups find attractive (such as few distractions and more business services), hence the customers decide that their productivity will be improved by staying an extra night. An examination of each sales rep will be required to determine if changes are warranted, particularly given Sale Rep 2's performance, or if each is already maximizing their potential given the kind of territory each has. The four-factor model provides direction for sales management on where to look next to improve performance.

Industrial-selling cycles are longer and more complex than their consumer-selling counterparts, so each of the four factors will have a different baseline performance from that shown in the illustration. But the impact on decision making will be similar since sales management will compare the results to other sales people on their team, or against competitors and/or industry standards.

Endnotes

[1] Cron, W. L., T. E. DeCarlo and D. J. Palrymple. *Sales Management,* John Wiley & Sons, Inc., 2004: p. 545.

[2] Adapted from information provided by Northwest Resorts, Inc.

Additional References

Davis, J. *Measuring Marketing: 103 Key Metrics Every Marketer Needs,* John Wiley & Sons (Asia) Pte Ltd., 2007.

www.faculty.bus.olemiss.edu/dvorhies/Sales%20Management/Powerpoint%20Slides/ch13.ppt.ppt

46 Sales–Variance Analysis

The Definition

Sales-variance analysis incorporates the methodologies used to measure deviations between sales plan and actual performance.

The Formulas and Their Components[1]

There are several formulas that can be used to calculate sales variances. We will concentrate on the three most commonly used to assess sales performance:

- Value variance

- Price variance

- Volume variance.

Sales-value variance

This measures the difference in monetary value between actual sales and budgeted sales (in monetary terms) in a given time period (usually one year).

$$SV_{al}V_t = S_{at} - S_b$$

Where

$SV_{al}V_t$ = sales-value variance during time t
S_{at} = actual sales during time t
S_b = budgeted sales

If actual sales are more than budgeted sales, then this formula will return a favorable variance. Whether positive or negative, sales managers will want to determine the source of this variance. If the variance is positive, then it is due either to higher actual prices compared to budget, or higher actual volume compared to budget. The converse would be true if the variance were negative. With price as one of the determinants, sales management would now want to measure the sales-price variance.

Sales-price variance

The sales-price variance describes the difference between actual price received and the price budgeted at the beginning of the set period.

$$SPV_t = Q_a(P_a - P_b)$$

Where

SPV_t = sales-price variance during time t
Q_a = actual quantity sold during time t
P_a = actual price per unit
P_b = budgeted price per unit

Actual price differences result from promotional or volume discounts, allowances, giveaways, or bundled offerings (such as two-for-one deals), all of which are used by sales people to gain a buyer's commitment. Correspondingly, their use affects the final price received.

Note: Magic Number 47 provides a more detailed example of calculating sales-price variance.

Sales-volume variance

Sales-volume variance measures the difference in actual quantity sold during time t versus the budgeted quantity, multiplied by the budgeted price per unit.

$$SVV_t = P_b(Q_a - Q_b)$$

Where

SVV_t = sales-volume variance during time t
P_b = budgeted price per unit

Q_a = actual quantity sold during time t
Q_b = budgeted quantity sold during time t

Sales-volume variances are caused by several factors. Changes in price or quality, delivery delays, shifting market trends and competitor promotions are among the key influences. Marketers and sales management must review sales results closely to understand the source of the variances.

*Note: Magic Number 48 describes another approach to evaluating sales-volume variance.

WHERE'S THE DATA?

Each of the sales-variance formulas comprises budgeted and actual figures. The budgeted amounts are based on the company's overall strategic goals for the time period in question, usually one year, which each department then incorporates into its own business plans for its employees. The budgeted sales figures for sales-value variance are based on results from previous time periods, with an emphasis on the most recent, plus growth targets for the upcoming period. The budgeted price per unit for both price and volume variance is based on the recent period's pricing, plus an expected cost increase from suppliers or for inflation. The budgeted quantity used in sales-volume variance is also a combination of historical quantities and an allowance for planned increases, which themselves reflect the approximate volume growth changes from previous periods.

The actual figures for each formula come from the end-of-period review of financial performance.

CALCULATING IT

To illustrate value, price and volume variance, let's assume that Company A sells three products, known as X, Y and Z, respectively. Company A budgeted the following sales for 2005:

Budgeted Sales for 2005

Product X:100,000 units sold at $25 each = $2,500,000
Product Y: 50,000 units sold at $30 each = $1,500,000
Product Z: 25,000 units sold at $35 each = $875,000
Budgeted sales   **$4,875,000**

Actual Sales for 2005

Product X: 90,000 units sold at $28 each = $2,520,000
Product Y: 45,000 units sold at $32 each = $1,440,000
Product Z: 30,000 units sold at $34 each = $1,020,000
Actual sales   **$4,980,000**

The next step is to examine the variances in sales value, sales price and sales volume.

Company A had a favorable sales-value variance. In this case, the actual sales of all three products exceeded the budgeted amount by $105,000, shown as follows:

$SV_{al}V_t$ $= S_a - S_b$
$SV_{al}V_t$ $= \$4,980,000 - \$4,875,000$
Sales-value variance   **= $105,000**

The sales-price variance for each product shows the following:

Product X = 90,000 (28 − 25)   = $270,000
Product Y = 45,000 (32 −30)   = $90,000
Product Z = 30,000 (34 − 35)   = ($30,000)
Sales-price variance   **= $330,000**

The overall SPV was favorable, but whereas Products X and Y had favorable individual SPVs, Product Z had an unfavorable variance.

The sales-volume variance for each product shows the following:

Product X = $25 (90,000 − 100,000) = ($250,000)
Product Y = $30 (45,000 − 50,000)   = ($150,000)
Product Z = $35 (30,000 − 25,000)   = $175,000
Sales-volume variance   **($225,000)**

The overall SVV was unfavorable. Products X and Y both had unfavorable SVVs, but Product Z had a favorable variance.

A quick check of the sales-price variance and sales-volume variance should verify the sales-value variance figure:

Sales price variance	$330,000
Sales volume variance	($225,000)
Total variance	**$105,000**

Sales-mix variance

There is another method for calculating sales variances known as the "sales-mix variance", which measures the impact of different mixes of product sold. This is useful for companies with multiple products and product lines where management needs to understand the financial implications to the company of the actual product mix sold vis-à-vis the budgeted product mix. The formula for this is:

$$SMV_t = Q_t \, (A\% - B\%) \, CM_b$$

Where

SMV_t = sales-mix variance during time t
Q_t = actual quantity (in units) of all products sold in time t
$A\%$ = actual sales-mix percentage
$B\%$ = budgeted sales-mix percentage
CM_b = budgeted contribution margin per unit

What It Means and Potential Challenges

Sales managers develop budgets for their business plans that outline how the department's money is going to be allocated between revenues and costs for a specific period of time, usually for the forthcoming year. Once the year has been completed, the actual financial performance is compared to the original budget.

Sales-variance analysis enables company management to identify the impact of specific variables on overall sales performance. If management reviewed only total sales results, then they would conclude that the business performed better than plan (using the example we looked at above). But the sales-variance analysis sheds light on the performance of individual products. Interestingly, Products X and Y had favorable sales-price variances, but unfavorable sales-volume variances (the actual prices for which the products sold more than offset the lower-than-expected unit sales). Conversely, Product Z had an unfavorable sales-price variance as a result of the lower actual price for which products were sold, but it also had a favorable sales-volume variance.

Company management would want to carefully review the reasons for these performance swings. All three products are somewhat price elastic, meaning that customers are sensitive to price changes. Perhaps the competition offers equivalent products to X and Y, but at better prices. Therefore management might consider either improving product quality or finding ways to reduce costs. The small price decrease for Product Z (less than 3%) led to a 20% increase in units sold (30,000 actual as opposed to the 25,000 budgeted) and a positive sales-volume variance of $175,000. Furthermore, the actual sales of Product Z were $145,000 higher than budgeted ($1,020,000 actual vs. $875,000 budgeted), a 16.6% increase in sales. For Product Z, the 3% price decrease resulted in a disproportionate, positive percentage increase in sales-volume variance and actual sales. Sales management would want to analyze these results more closely to understand better why Product Z's results were superior to those of Products X and Y and determine whether similar results might be replicated in the future.

There are many reasons for these results beyond the simple explanations offered here. Sales-variance analysis provides meaningful insight into businesses performance. While it raises more questions for management, it also offers guidance on where to look for the answers.

Endnote

[1] http://www.rcw.raifoundation.org/management/mba/Financial&Management Accounting/lecture-notes/lecture-28.pdf&lecture-29.pdf

Additional References

Davis, J. *Measuring Marketing: 103 Key Metrics Every Marketer Needs,* John Wiley & Sons (Asia) Pte Ltd., 2007.

http://www.google.com/search?q=%22sales+volume+variance%22+definition&hl= en&lr=&start=10&sa=N

http://www.freeworldacademy.com/newbizzadviser/fw29.htm

http://www.maaw.info/Chapter13.htm#Part%20I.%20Alternative%20Four%20 Variance%20with%20Sales%20Mix

http://www.prenticehall.ca/horngren/horngren_cost_3/ppt/teall_cost_3_ch16.ppt#2 59,6,Sales-Mix and Sales-Quantity Variance

47

Sales-Price Variance

THE DEFINITION

This Magic Number expands on the sales-price variance methodology introduced in Magic Number 46. Sales-price variance measures the difference between the recommended or retail price and the actual, final, selling price. It occurs as a result of changes in customer demand, unexpected shifts in market conditions and the actions of competitors.

THE FORMULA AND ITS COMPONENTS[1]

The formula for calculating sales-price variance is:

$$SPV_t = Q_a(P_a - P_b)$$

Where

SPV_t = sales-price variance during time t
Q_a = actual quantity sold in time period t
P_a = actual price per unit
P_b = budgeted price per unit

WHERE'S THE DATA?

The figures for actual units sold and actual price received come from end-of-period financial reviews and performance evaluations after all adjustments (discounts, lost shipments, and so on) are included. The budgeted or retail price (see Magic Numbers 13–15 on pricing) is determined from a combination of current product costs, previous pricing, competitors' pricing, and product positioning needs.

CALCULATING IT

To illustrate, let's say Glob Toys sells a product called "BlobSlob" which is a shiny, clay-like substance that kids mold into monster shapes. The company sold 100,000 units last year at an actual price of $4 each. The suggested retail price was $5.

$$SPV = 100,000 \times (\$4 - \$5)$$

$$= -\$100,000$$

The calculation shows that Glob Toys had an SPV of −$100,000, meaning that actual sales were lower than projected sales by that amount. Let's look at a more sophisticated treatment: Glob Toys has two products, BlobSlob and SlobberChops (a toy dog with a perpetual drool). Glob planned its expected results as follows:

Projected performance

	BlobSlob	SlobberChops
Unit sales (projected)	100,000	50,000
Unit price (recommended)	$5	$10
Unit cost (projected)	$3	$6

Actual performance

	BlobSlob	SlobberChops
Unit sales (actual)	120,000	60,000
Unit price (actual)	$4	$8.50
Unit cost (actual)	$3	$6

In this case, costs remain the same because Glob Toys had locked in supplier prices and production costs in advance. We can now compare:

Projected revenue $(100,000 \times \$5) + (50,000 \times \$10) = \$1,000,000$

Actual revenue $(120,000 \times \$4) + (60,000 \times \$8.50) = \$990,000$

Projected profit $(100,000 \times \$2) + (50,000 \times \$4)$ $= \$400,000$

Actual profit $(120,000 \times \$1) + (60,000 \times \$1.50) = \$210,000$

Total sales variance $= -\$190,000$

The next step is to calculate the SPV:

$$SPV = \{120,000 \times (\$4 - \$5)\} + \{60,000 \times (\$8.50 - \$10.00)\}$$

$$= -\$210,000$$

Therefore, Glob Toys' sales-price variance shows the effect of price changes from projected to actual, resulting in a shortfall in total sales of $210,000 against the original plan.

WHAT IT MEANS AND POTENTIAL CHALLENGES

In this example, management would have to decide if the reduction in price for both products, which led to a greater number of units sold than allowed for in the original plan, was warranted, given the reduction in overall revenues and profits. Perhaps the increase in unit volume sold was part of management's longer-term plan, since the additional units may signal a larger overall customer base buying the company's products, which could yield higher revenues and profits in future years. Conversely, management may decide that the increase in units sold was not sufficient justification for the reduced revenues and profits.

While it is clear that price changes have an impact on actual financial performance, it is less obvious how to fix it in the future. The marketer could mandate a strict "no discounting" policy, with the CEO and CFO's blessings, no doubt. Some consumers would likely pay the full amount, but many more would simply shift to a competing product or delay purchase to a later time. This would exacerbate the sales-variance problem since there would now be a smaller customer base *and* lower sales, not to mention a probable negative perception of Glob Toys' image, particularly from retailers who want to sell the inventory quickly. Retail customers may reduce their future purchases of Glob Toys' products, believing that the firm is inflexible and insensitive to their needs and the market conditions that created them.

Marketers in this situation have several options:

- Hold firm on price and risk reduced overall sales and a smaller customer base

- Allow pricing deviations to attract more customers, but recognize that lower sales and reduced margins will result. This may increase market share for a short time, but it may also lock in a more permanent lower-margin performance

- Reduce costs to allow for greater pricing flexibility without eroding margins

- Increase the value-add of the products, perhaps by offering a unique loyalty program or a clear explanation of why their product is superior and why it is relevant to the customer.

None of these are easy choices and a marketer may try each in an effort to find the best combination that maximizes sales and profits, and attracts the largest number of customers.

Endnote

[1]Gilligan, C. and R. M. S. Wilson. *Strategic Marketing Management: Planning, Implementation & Control*, Elsevier Butterworth-Heinemann 2005: p. 781.

Additional Reference

Davis, J. *Measuring Marketing: 103 Key Metrics Every Marketer Needs*, John Wiley & Sons (Asia) Pte Ltd., 2007.

Sales–Volume Variance

THE DEFINITION

Sales-volume variance describes the difference between projected and actual sales volume results.

Magic Number 46 introduced sales-variance analysis, including an alternative to sales-volume variance. Magic Number 47 expanded on sales-price variance introduced in Magic Number 46, which helps marketers understand how price changes affect actual sales. Here, we provide a modified approach to sales-volume variance that uses sales-quantity variance and sales-mix variances as the two variables (whereas Magic Number 47 used budgeted price, actual price and actual quantity as the variables). Readers will note that the factors that determine sales-mix variance (projected and expected profits from actual sales) and sales-quantity variance (projected profit based on projected sales and expected profit from actual sales) are similar, although not identical, measures.

THE FORMULA AND ITS COMPONENTS[1]

Sales-volume variance is calculated using the following formula:

$$SVV_t = SQV_t + SMV_t$$

Where

SVV_t = sales-volume variance in time period t
SQV_t = sales-quantity variance in time period t
SMV_t = sales-mix variance in time period t

To be able to complete this, the marketer first needs to calculate SQV and SMV, as follows:

$$SQV_t = PPPS_t - EPAS_t$$

Where

SQV_t = sales-quantity variance in time period t
$PPPS_t$ = projected profit based on projected sales in time period t
$EPAS_t$ = expected profit from actual sales in time period t*

*calculated as though profit increases or decreases proportionately with changes in the level of sales[2]

$$SMV_t = EPAS_t - PPAS_t$$

Where

SMV_t = sales-mix variance in time period t
$EPAS_t$ = expected profit from actual sales in time period t
$PPAS_t$ = projected profit from actual sales in time period t**

**sum of projected profit for all units sold[3]

WHERE'S THE DATA?

The projected profits figure is a combination of historical quantities plus an allowance for planned growth. The growth is determined based on previous period-over-period growth patterns, together with subjective factors based on sales management's understanding of current market conditions. Expected profit from actual sales is derived from actual sales performance. Increased or decreased sales affects profits proportionately in the same direction.

The actual figures for each formula come from the review of financial performance at the end of the period.

CALCULATING IT

Returning to the Glob Toys example from Magic Number 47, we can now compute the results:

$$SQV_t = \$400,000 - (\$990,000 \div \$1,000,000 \times \$400,000)$$
$$= \$4,000$$

$$SMV_t = \$400,000 - \{(120,000 \times \$2) + (50,000 \times \$4)\}$$

$$= -\$40,000$$

The sales-volume variance can then be calculated:

$$SVV_t = \$4,000 + (-\$40,000)$$

$$= -\$36,000$$

Total sales variance

Using the results from Magic Number 47, the marketer can now calculate total sales variance:

$$TSV_t = SPV_t + SVV_t$$

$$= -\$210,000 + (-\$36,000)$$

$$= -\$246,000$$

WHAT IT MEANS AND POTENTIAL CHALLENGES

Several factors affect sales-volume variance:

- Customers' needs changed, resulting in an increase/decrease in quantity ordered

  Shifting customer needs are difficult to anticipate, even with the most thoroughly developed customer relationship. The customer's business conditions are affected by many factors beyond the control of the current buyer-seller relationship and cannot be anticipated completely. Sales management must create the conditions for an open relationship with customers so that potential quantity disruptions from such changes are minimized. Increased quantities can be just as challenging as decreases since the heightened demand affects production schedules, relationships with suppliers, logistics and shipping. Each of these can have a negative financial impact, despite the increase in quantity ordered.

- Unexpected cost increases forced an increase in price during time period t

  The sales team's customer leads should be regularly reported to sales management and to the operations and production departments, even though orders have yet to be confirmed. This is to prepare other areas of the company for anticipated orders and for any unusual requests the customer may have. As customers move through the sales cycle toward closure, the sales team must alert their production and operations counterparts, informing these departments of the likely quantities to be ordered. Working with other departments throughout the sales cycle, rather than at the end when orders are confirmed, minimizes surprises and enables the rest of the company to secure the best possible prices from suppliers, keeping costs as low as possible.

- Competitors introduced a new product that attracted customers away

New offerings from competitors may affect a customer's orders, even at the last minute. While no remedy is perfect, the sales team's success is predicated once again on having committed relationships with customers so that any hint of a move to a competitor is discussed between the buyer and seller. Open relationships contribute to minimizing this type of disruption. The sales team also has an obligation to learn as much as possible about competitors to reduce the possibility of being surprised by any new offerings.

- Production delays forced competitors to cancel commitments

If customers' orders increase significantly and there is little advance indication from the sales team, this can result in production delays which, in turn, can lead to customer dissatisfaction and canceled commitments. Sales management's responsibility is to develop the most professional sales team possible — from hiring, through training and ongoing on-the-job practice — so that each sales person fully understands the importance of early and thorough communication inside the company.

The implications differ for each of these factors and marketers will need to adjust their plans accordingly to ensure their products perform closer to expectations.

Endnotes

[1] Gilligan, C. and R. M. S. Wilson. *Strategic Marketing Management: Planning, Implementation & Control*, Elsevier Butterworth-Heinemann 2005: pp. 781–783.
[2] Ibid
[3] Ibid

Additional Reference

Davis, J. *Measuring Marketing: 103 Key Metrics Every Marketer Needs,* John Wiley & Sons (Asia) Pte Ltd., 2007.

MAGIC
NUM8ER

49

Sales Premiums

THE DEFINITION

Sales premiums are promotional items given to prospective customers as an incentive to purchase a product or service. Examples include coffee mugs, pens, t-shirts, Post-it® pads, mouse pads, glow sticks, magnetic business cards, toasters, and so on. The only limit to these is the imagination of the marketer and the relevance to the target product to be sold. Marketers use messages such as "Free Gift with Purchase" to generate interest in the product and its corresponding sales premium.

THE FORMULA AND ITS COMPONENTS

There is no formula for sales premiums, although it would be helpful to conduct a break-even analysis (discussed in Magic Number 27) since the premiums add cost to the marketing of a product or service and, therefore, must be actively considered if it is a necessary tool for inducing customers to purchase. The use of sales premiums must be evaluated with the same scrutiny used to determine the attractiveness of advertising, direct mail or promotional discounts since each of these, while inspiring an increase in sales, incurs additional costs and, therefore, reduces margins. Readers should note that the usage of sales premiums is one of many tools marketers use to influence sales of a key product or service.

WHERE'S THE DATA?

The data for sales premiums is based on the per-unit cost of the premium items used and the quantity ordered for the promotion. This information is easily acquired from suppliers specializing in promotional items. Sales management should pay attention to quantity discounts because per-unit costs decline as quantities ordered increase. But the key consideration is whether the use of the premiums results in a direct increase in sales of the product or service being promoted. If not, then the costs incurred to acquire the premiums simply add unnecessary expense to the overall sales and marketing effort.

CALCULATING IT

Marketers should calculate a break-even level for units sold without the sales premium, then factor in the cost of the premium to determine the new break-even level. If the marketer's judgment suggests that the break-even level is achievable with the inclusion of the sales premium, then it should be used.

WHAT IT MEANS AND POTENTIAL CHALLENGES

When planning growth opportunities, marketers need to determine how to generate new or renewed interest in their products. This includes considering the advantages and disadvantages of offering a gift or bonus if the consumer chooses to purchase, vis-à-vis advertising.

Years ago, some banks in the United States would offer a free appliance (such as a toaster) as a premium or incentive to attract new customers. The appliance cost the banks little if a customer actually opened an account and stayed with the bank for a minimum period, during which the bank could generate income from fees, interest charges and other services used by the customer. The upfront cost was higher than the initial benefit because there was not a one-to-one relationship between the number of appliances acquired on behalf of the promotion and the number of new customers who opened an account directly as a result. Nevertheless, this form of sales premium served to bring in customers.

More recent examples include video-game consoles and bundled games. The product to be sold is the console, but the bundled games are the premium added to encourage purchase. The games provided free with purchase are rarely the most popular games. But the premium succeeds because a customer who acquires the console (and the free game) learns to enjoy playing and returns to the retailer to buy more games. The marketer effectively creates an ongoing revenue stream from each customer acquired by this program, assuming the customer is a dedicated gamer. The reason for this is simple: the premium game inspired the purchase of the console; playing the console then inspired the purchase of more games; as new games are subsequently introduced, the customer's desire for these grows as well and leads to more purchases. Furthermore, premiums can be useful in attracting "premium customers" — customers who become loyal to the product or company. The marketer's challenge is in forecasting demand accurately enough to "know" that the cost of the premium is paid for by the sales of the targeted product — hence the need to calculate break-even before running the promotion.

Marketers will argue, with some justification, that even if sales do not increase as a direct result of the premium, there is the potential for a longer-term, positive impact since the premium often becomes a permanent fixture at the customer's office. With the marketer's logo or some other memorable icon clearly printed on the item, the repeated use of a premium such as a coffee mug results in the marketer's company being regularly exposed to users of that coffee mug. Measuring this indirect impact, however, is challenging.

References

American Marketing Association: http://www.marketingpower.com/mg-dictionary-view2483.php

Davis, J. *Magic Numbers for Consumer Marketing*, John Wiley & Sons (Asia) Pte Ltd., 2005: pp. 207–212.

Davis, J. *Measuring Marketing: 103 Key Metrics Every Marketer Needs,* John Wiley & Sons (Asia) Pte Ltd., 2007.

Imber, J. and B. Toffler. *Dictionary of Marketing Terms*, Barron's Educational Series, Inc., 2000: p. 433.

Kotler, P., M. L. Siew, H. A. Swee, and C. T. Tan, *Marketing Management:* A Strategic Perspective, Prentice Hall Pearson Education Asia Pte Ltd., 2003: p. 654.

MAGIC NUMBER 50

Return On Sales

THE DEFINITION

Businesses must have sales to survive and profits to thrive. To thrive, the quality of the sales must be understood. Return on sales measures profitability and is defined as the amount of profit produced relative to each dollar of sales.

THE FORMULA AND ITS COMPONENTS

Return on sales (ROS) is a measure of a company's ability to generate profits from sales. It is effectively the profit resulting from each dollar of sales and is based on profit before tax and total sales.[1] It is represented as follows:

$$ROS = \frac{P_{bt}}{S}$$

Where

ROS = return on sales
P_{bt} = profit before tax
S   = sales (in dollars)

WHERE'S THE DATA?

ROS data is found in the income statement where its main components are recorded.

Figures 50.1 and 50.2 are the income statements for Google, Inc[2] and Toyota respectively for the years 2003, 2004 and 2005.[2] In this example, the line item called "total revenue" equates to "sales (in dollars)" in the formula above, and "income before tax" is the equivalent of the "profit before tax" variable.

Figure 50.1   Google, Inc. income statements 2003–2006

PERIOD ENDING	31-Dec-05	31-Dec-04	31-Dec-03
Total Revenue	6,138,560	3,189,223	1,465,934
Cost of Revenue	2,577,088	1,457,653	625,854
Gross Profit	3,561,472	1,731,570	840,080
Operating Expenses			
Research Development	599,510	225,632	91,228
Selling General and Administrative	854,684	664,746	406,388
Non-recurring	90,000	201,000	—
Others	—	—	—
Total Operating Expenses	—	—	—
Operating Income or Loss	2,017,278	640,192	342,464
Income from Continuing Operations			
Total Other Income/Expenses Net	125,175	10,904	6,121
Earnings Before Interest and Taxes	2,142,453	651,096	348,585
Interest Expense	776	862	1,931
Income Before Tax	2,141,677	650,234	346,654
Income Tax Expense	676,280	251,115	241,006
Minority Interest	—	—	—
Net Income From Continuing Ops	1,465,397	399,119	105,648
Non-recurring Events			
Discontinued Operations	—	—	—
Extraordinary Items	—	—	—
Effect of Accounting Changes	—	—	—
Other Items	—	—	—
Net Income	1,465,397	399,119	105,648
Preferred Stock and Other Adjustments	—	—	—
Net Income Applicable To Common Shares	$1,465,397	$399,119	$105,648

Figure 50.2   Toyota Corporation income statements 2003–2005

PERIOD ENDING	31-Mar-05	31-Mar-04	31-Mar-03
Total Revenue	172,749,000	163,637,000	128,965,000
Cost of Revenue	138,469,000	131,238,000	102,647,000
Gross Profit	34,280,000	32,399,000	26,318,000
Operating Expenses			
Research Development	—	—	—
Selling General and Administrative	18,709,000	16,627,000	15,739,000
Non-recurring	—	—	—
Others	—	—	—
Total Operating Expenses	—	—	—
Operating Income or Loss	15,571,000	15,772,000	10,579,000
Income from Continuing Operations			
Total Other Income/Expenses Net	945,000	1,131,000	(121,000)
Earnings Before Interest and Taxes	16,516,000	16,903,000	10,458,000
Interest Expense	177,000	196,000	253,000
Income Before Tax	16,339,000	16,707,000	10,205,000
Income Tax Expense	6,126,000	6,446,000	4,301,000
Minority Interest	(605,000)	(404,000)	(96,000)
Net Income From Continuing Ops	10,907,000	10,995,000	6,247,000
Non-recurring Events			
Discontinued Operations	—	—	—
Extraordinary Items	—	—	—
Effect of Accounting Changes	—	—	—
Other Items	—	—	—
Net Income	10,907,000	10,995,000	6,247,000
Preferred Stock and Other			
Adjustments	—	—	—
Net Income Applicable To			
Common Shares	$10,907,000	$10,995,000	$6,247,000

CALCULATING IT

The ROS figures for both companies over the three years can be calculated as follows:

Google

- In 2003, revenues were $1.466 billion and its profit before tax was $346,654.

$$\text{ROS} = \frac{\$347 \text{ k}}{\$1.466 \text{ b}} = 23.7\%$$

- In 2004, revenues were $3.189 billion and its profit before tax was $650,234.

$$\text{ROS} = \frac{\$650 \text{ k}}{\$3.189 \text{ b}} = 20.4\%$$

- In 2005, revenues were $6.139 billion and its profit before tax was $2.142 billion.

$$\text{ROS} = \frac{\$2.142 \text{ b}}{\$6.139 \text{ b}} = 34.9\%$$

Toyota

- In 2003, revenues were $129 billion and its profit before tax was $10.2 billion.

$$\text{ROS} = \frac{\$10.2 \text{ b}}{\$129 \text{ b}} = 7.9\%$$

- In 2004, revenues were $163.6 billion and its profit before tax was $16.7 billion.

$$\text{ROS} = \frac{\$16.7 \text{ b}}{\$163.6 \text{ b}} = 10.2\%$$

- In 2005, revenues were $172.7 billion and its profit before tax was $16.3 billion.

$$\text{ROS} = \frac{\$16.3 \text{ b}}{\$172.7 \text{ b}} = 9.4\%$$

Each company's ROS is different from that of any other and even from its own performance over preceding years. Closer examination of Google's and Toyota's respective markets may reveal that the respective returns shown are reasonable given the competitive conditions in which they each operate. To know for certain, marketers need to understand the market in which they compete and the relative performance of their main competitors. If their competitors have recorded an ROS in a similar range, then each company may appear to be performing well.

Let's consider this in relation to Google's case, where Yahoo! is considered a competitor. Yahoo!'s 2005 revenues were $5.2 billion and its profit before tax was $2.5 billion, resulting in an ROS of 48%.[4] By comparison, Google's ROS of 34% may seem *low*. However, the nature of the industry in which they compete is uneven, so the discrepancies may be explainable. Furthermore, Google does not have the same business model as Yahoo!, each using different approaches to developing their markets. So is the ROS comparison fair or, for that matter, relevant? To a certain extent, yes, as long as management is aware of the vagaries associated with competitive comparisons.

The same is true with Toyota. Its biggest competitor in sales and market share is General Motors (GM). GM's 2005 revenues were $192.6 billion and its profit before tax was −$16.9 billion (i.e. GM lost money). Its ROS was −8.8%.[5] By comparison, therefore, Toyota's ROS would appear to be reasonable. On the other hand, GM has different cost structures and has been struggling for years to make the company more competitive. Perhaps each company's ROS is reasonable given their respective situations.

Let's look at a more general industry example. Figure 50.3 shows the ROS for the consumer-electronic games and toys market in the United States for the years 2002, 2003 and 2004.[6]

It is noteworthy that in 2003, the industry's collective ROS declined 11.3%. This may suggest several influencing factors reflecting shifts in industry dynamics:

- Perhaps fewer new products were introduced, leading to a decline in interest in this category.

- Conversely, perhaps several new products were introduced that were not well received by consumers, compelling companies to drop prices to clear inventory and, temporarily, reducing their profits.

Figure 50.3   ROS for U.S. consumer-electronic games and toys, 2002–2004

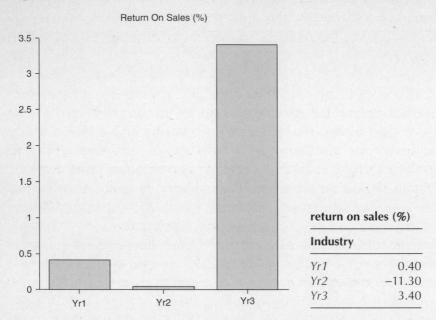

return on sales (%)	
Industry	
Yr1	0.40
Yr2	−11.30
Yr3	3.40

- Prices for new products may have been too high, causing consumer resistance.

- There may have been a dramatic shift in consumer interest in this category of products in general, perhaps away from packaged games and toward online games.

Further investigation would undoubtedly provide clues as to the factors that led to the ROS results shown here.

WHAT IT MEANS AND POTENTIAL CHALLENGES

ROS is a practical indicator of the profitability of a company's marketing efforts. It is used most effectively when reviewed over time, rather than for a single period, since it enables departures from historical and industry trends to be detected.

In the earlier examples, as Google grows, it may want to focus more on diversifying its business model to take advantage of the more profitable revenue streams Yahoo! seems to generate. Google's growth has been extraordinary during this three-year stretch, with ROS improving dramatically. Yet so too has Yahoo!'s, with its ROS growing from 23% in 2003 to 33% in 2004. The growth solution for both companies is likely to be quite different because each has differing approaches to the market.

Return on sales measures the financial efficiency of a company's recent sales efforts, particularly in comparison to other companies in the same industry. ROS does vary significantly by industry and, at times, within industries. It can be a useful indicator of a given company's ability to respond to changes in its own operating performance, general market conditions or pricing. For example, an increase in return on sales may signal improved operational efficiency (i.e. lower expenses). On the other hand, it may reflect a change in a company's pricing strategy. Therefore, marketers should investigate further before drawing conclusions based on initial ROS results. Higher prices may have led to the increased return on sales; but are the increased prices sustainable over the long term? Is the company adding sufficient value to justify the increased price? Whatever the reasons, ROS results should provoke additional curiosity and inquiry if marketers wish to understand the reasons behind the figures.

Endnotes

[1] ROS can also be calculated based on P_{nat} (net profit *after* tax). Whether before-tax or after-tax profits are used, the convention should be applied consistently across all return ratios (ROA, ROE). The formula is as follows:

$$ROS = \frac{P_{nat}}{S}$$

[2] http://finance.yahoo.com/q/is?s=GOOG&annual
[3] http://finance.yahoo.com/q/is?s=TM&annual
[4] http://finance.yahoo.com/q/is?s=YHOO&annual
[5] http://finance.yahoo.com/q?s=gm
[6] BizMiner, The Brandow Company, 2005, report on Consumer Electronic Games and Toys Market, http://www.bizminer.com/search/details/industries/Electronicgames-and-toys-Manufacturing.asp?profile=SMI&showALL=1

Additional References

Best, R. J. *Market-Based Management: Strategies for Growing Customer Value and Profitability*, Upper Saddle River, New Jersey: Pearson Education Inc., 2005: p. 478.

Davis, J. *Magic Numbers for Consumer Marketing*, John Wiley & Sons (Asia) Pte Ltd., 2005: pp. 69–70.

Davis, J. *Measuring Marketing: 103 Key Metrics Every Marketer Needs,* John Wiley & Sons (Asia) Pte Ltd., 2007.

http://www.investopedia.com/terms/r/ros.asp

http://prosearch.businessweek.com/businessweek/GENERAL_FREE_SEARCH.html?Button=Description&CRITERIA=038

Index

Other Titles in the
MAG1C NUM8ERS Series...

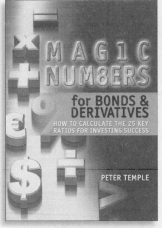

With investment choices becoming broader, savvy investors need to know not just about stocks, but also about bonds and derivatives. This book is the first real attempt to explain the inner workings of these alternative investment choices.

0-470-82139-6
November 2004

An excellent reference guide to the key quantitative assessment tools for HR practitioners. This book simply outlines a range of the key measures that any HR, financial or business manager can use to address this situation in a more business-like manner.

0-470-82161-2
October 2005

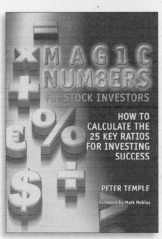

This book looks at key ratios that all investors can use easily to look at the financial health and growth prospects of a company before they buy shares in it. The ratios are described in details, with simple formulas, and help on where to find the data needed to calculate them.

0-470-82124-8
September 2003

Magic Numbers for Consumer Marketing is the ideal resource for marketers and company leaders who wish to better understand their marketing efforts. If you are interested in gaining a truly competitive edge, then this is the book you need to succeed.

0-470-82162-0
July 2005

Magic Numbers is the essential guide to making objective judgements about companies and their shares. If you don't want to see your money cut in half or vanish altogether, we strongly recommend you read this book.

0-471-47924-1
August 2001